Efw

ENCOURAGEMENT
for your
identity

A 30 Day Devotional
by Women for Women

Dedication

Most men will proclaim every one his own goodness: but a faithful man who can find? – Proverbs 20:6

Neal, God allowed me to meet you only after I was fully content in being His child and nothing more. The joy found in knowing who we are in Christ alone is like no other. I'm so thankful for your patience with me as we followed the Lord's leading in our developing relationship.

I love you! I love your faithfulness to Jesus! I love that every morning without fail I can walk into your prayer closet at 5:00 A.M. and find you on your knees praying for those Christ loves.

From every vacation, to every lazy family day wrestling with the kids on the living room floor, you lead our family with faithfulness and conviction.

I have no doubt that whatever comes our way you will remain faithful to our Savior because you rest in knowing that you are His. Thank you for your love, your leadership, and your faithfulness. You are my forever favorite!

Love you most!
Charity

Praise for Encouragement From Women Who've Been There

Encouragement From Women Who've Been There is a ministry I truly love. Authenticity is something many long for in life and often struggle to find. When you are in the midst of life's storms, challenging or lonely times, there is no better substitute than to connect with those who seek to please God and to whom you can relate — to those who have been there and understand what you are feeling or experiencing. We can find purpose in all seasons of our lives if we look to God for His purpose in them. The real-life women in these devotionals are those authentic Christian ladies who have been there, and whom God is using to encourage you today. As you journey through life in a world of uncertainty and so much lacking in authenticity, they are pointing you toward Jesus. I am confident that whatever encouragement you need from other Christian women you will find in the pages of this devotional!

Deberah Costillo - Founder and President of Las Vegas Metro Police Officer Wives; Founder and President of Polices Wives of America; - Interim Executive Director/Board Member, First Choice Pregnancy Services

Get your coffee, get in your favorite chair, and give yourself a few moments in volume II of EFW, *Encouragement For Your Identity*. Your heart will be blessed and secured in the truth shared concerning your identity. Glean the wisdom written in these chapters for yourself and for a society that needs to know "who" and "why" we are. I love being Doug's wife, Clint's mom, along with many other identity descriptors, but it is knowing that I am a daughter of The King, Psalm 45:9, that equips me and secures me for today and for eternity.

Kathleen A. Jackson - Ladies Event Speaker and Author of *All This...and Heaven too*, Mother of three, grandma to five. Lead Pastor's wife at Community Baptist Church, Saginaw Michigan

There is nothing sweeter than hearing a Word of encouragement from the Lord at the exact moment you need it most. That's what EFW is to me. It's an army of Christian women from all walks of life sharing truth from God's Word and lessons from life that soothe the soul. Through online ministry and now printed devotionals, your heart will be uplifted and encouraged through the words of EFW devotionals. In a world where hearts are hurting and pulled in every direction, EFW points the heart back to God's Word. You are sure to be encouraged!

Micah Maddox – Ladies Event Speaker and Author of *Anchored In: Experience a Power-Full Life in a Problem-Filled World*, Mother of four and foster mom

"Encouragement is the transfer of strength!" My loving friend includes these supportive words in every card she mails! Ladies, no one can successfully traverse life's challenging and ever changing road alone. Join the precious "life coach" ladies at the EFW blog to find your heart blessed and ready to transfer your newfound strength to a fellow pilgrim!

Miriam Cummins Marriott – "Campus Mom" and wife to the President at Maranatha Baptist University. Miriam is a ladies conference speaker, mother to three, and grandmother of twelve

Reading EFW is like travelling on a journey with a close companion. Each author writes from her heart, saying exactly what I need to hear. The Lord has used EFW in my life so many times to encourage me as I travel the bumpy roads of busyness, discouragement, trials, triumphs, ministry, family and more, receiving biblical and practical helps along the way. God is so good to allow us to travel alongside other Christians. You will also be blessed and encouraged along your journey through this devotional. Come alongside and let's travel together because *"two are better than one"* Ecclesiastes 4:9-10.

Sharon Rabon – Author, ladies event speaker, Pastor's Wife/Director of Ladies' Ministries Beacon Baptist Church Raleigh, NC

At no time in my life have I met and talked with so many women who are just plain discouraged and searching for answers. This book of encouragement could be exactly what you need to give you hope and help in your daily walk with the Lord.

Mary Rice – Evangelist wife, ladies event speaker, together with her husband they have served in evangelism and Christian camp ministry of the Bill Rice Ranch close to 55 years

And let us consider one another to provoke unto love and to good works – Hebrews 10:24. I believe this Scripture displays the heart behind the ministry of EFW. I'm so thankful for the team of Christian women who have chosen to combine forces to fulfill the commission given to us in this passage. Women who range in age and backgrounds come together to help advance further the Kingdom work for the glory of God. If you want to be encouraged, dive into these devotionals with an open heart toward God. Ask Him to use these lessons to provoke your heart unto love and good works.

Anna Teis – Co-Founder/Lead Pastor's Wife of Liberty Baptist Church, home school pioneer, mother of five, grandma to eighteen

Special thanks to:

Tiffany Armstrong – Editor

Krystal Heath - Editor

Dan Kane - Editor

Heather Cusumano – Cover Design

ISBN: 9798495354937

Printed in the United States of America

Table of Contents

Encouragement From the Men Who Encourage Us

An Invitation to Contribute

Author Biographies

Additional Resources

A Final Word

Introduction

While compiling this devotional I was simultaneously compiling two others: one on marriage, the other on motherhood. Although these topics, too, are needed, the topic of identity seems to be a timely and reoccurring theme that is begging to be addressed.

We cannot reach our full God-directed potential as a mother, wife, or Christian unless we first understand who we are in Him. Therefore, I've put these two other works on pause so that we can get this guide into your hands first.

The women described in this devotional are not perfect and they'd be the first to tell you that they don't have all the answers, but they will point you to the Perfect One Who has every answer.

I'm excited for you to dive into this devotional guide! It is my prayer that you come to the pages of this book, as well as the other resources of *Encouragement From Women Who've Been There* [EFW], again and again to be reminded of whom you are in Christ. You are a new creation! Your circumstances do not define you. Jesus does!

Get ready to be encouraged in your identity!

Love in Christ,
~Charity

Week One

ENCOURAGEMENT FROM WOMEN

Identity
Charity Joy Berkey

Therefore if any man be in Christ, he is a new creature: old things are passed away; behold, all things are become new. - 2 Corinthians 5:17

I am crucified with Christ: nevertheless I life; yet not I, but Christ liveth in me: and the life which I now live in the flesh I live by the faith of the Son of God, who loved me, and gave himself for me. - Galatians 2:20

Who are you? Stop. Think about it. After musing over this question for a moment, go ahead and answer out loud, or write it out.

Look at your answer. Who do you think you are? Did you claim your talents? Maybe you mentioned your athletic ability or your occupation. "I'm a fitness coach." "I'm an ambassador for healthcare products."

Perhaps you claimed a relationship status? A girlfriend, wife, or mom? Some people are defined by a sin in their past. We see examples of this even in biblical heroines such as Rahab the Harlot.

How about what others label you? For the past 39 years I've been labeled "The Pastor's Daughter." Just last week a friend of mine introduced me as "The Pastor's Daughter." Although I've been married to my pastor husband for over 13 years, they still see me as "The Pastor's Daughter."

But that's not me.

My talents do not define me. My job does not define me. My family does not define me. The one and only relationship that eternally defines who I am is the relationship I have with Jesus Christ. And the exact same truth goes for you, too! We forget who Jesus says we are. Remember Him? The One Who created you, the One Who truly knows whom you were meant to be? He says you are brand spankin' new! You don't even belong here, you're not supposed to fit in.

If my identity is wrapped up in my motherhood, what happens when my kids grow up and move away? What about being a wife? Surely God doesn't want us to wrap up our identity in marriage. If you identify solely as a wife, the moment there is a disagreement with your spouse your identity is called into questioned.

Why do we have Christian women who struggle with their body image, who can't manage friendships, who hate some aspects of their lives? Can I suggest it's that we are Christians who are trying to live like those in the world? If you are a Christian you cannot be anything else. That, my friend, is who you are. That is what it boils down to. You are His!

When we care more about who we truly are and live out who we are meant to be, that's when we have freedom from caring about what ANYONE thinks of us. So do you want to crush these years God has given you? Do you want to LOVE being a woman or do you just want to survive? Let's get started by:

- Knowing who we are — we already established this one. We are His.

- Desire to be like Him — If you're reading this devotional and it wasn't forced upon you then you obviously have that desire.

- Learning to live out my faith — this, this right here is what most of us are missing. This is what is at the root of our insecurities, our downfalls, our despising of our own selves.

As I was writing this, I asked Cherish Grace, my then seven year old daughter, "Who are you?" Her very first answer was, "I'm God's Friend!" This is where our mindset should be. We can get there, but it doesn't happen overnight. It's going to require a change in thinking and, for some, major lifestyle changes. But it's more than worth it. Finding your identity and beginning to live it out now will save you a lifetime of heartache.

Ask the Holy Spirit right now to guide you. Ask Him to use this devotional to reveal His truth to you. Beg Him to help you experience His grace and strength to live out who you truly were meant to become, His friend, His representative, His beloved child.

Naked Fingers and a Broken Heart
Kimberly Joy

How precious also are thy thoughts unto me, O God! how great is the sum of them! If I should count them, they are more in number than the sand: when I awake, I am still with thee. -Psalm 139:17-18

I vividly remember the last day I wore my wedding rings. It was Sunday, August 31, 2014. That was the day that my life, marriage, home, and heart were shattered.

I had tried desperately to save my marriage. After discovering my husband's adultery, I begged God to change his heart and keep our family together. I prayed and pleaded, sobbing every night in the shower where no one could hear me. I endured years of bitterness and anger from my husband, hoping he would one day change.

He never did. That Sunday evening I discovered some things I wished had never happened. Things that meant there was no going back, no salvaging this marriage. Although I never wanted to be divorced, I had no other choice.

The events of the day were so traumatic that one of my closest friends, Tracey, wisely suggested my boys and I sleep at her house. Numb with pain, I agreed. I stood in my bedroom, unable to think clearly enough to pack an overnight bag.

Gently, Tracey listed the items I would need. Pajamas, socks, clothes for the morning. Brush and comb, deodorant, toothbrush, shoes…

I packed the bag, then paused before leaving my bedroom, what once had been our bedroom, the bedroom I would never again share with my husband.

Opening my jewelry box, I slipped off my rings and placed them inside. They would never again grace my finger.

In that moment I felt like the greater part of my identity had been stripped away. In time, "Mrs." would no longer be my identity. I would have to check the "divorced" box when filing out papers at the bank and doctor's office. I would have to explain why I lost my ministries, why my boys and I moved 10,000 miles from our home in Australia back to my native United States.

In the weeks that followed, I confessed to Tracy how strange my finger felt. Naked! It was almost like glancing down at a stranger's hands. Tracey decided to do something about it.

Shortly before my boys and I moved back to America, Tracy planned an overnight trip for the two of us on the gorgeous Australian coast. She booked a motel near the beach and took me to a beautiful restaurant overlooking the water.

Then she took me shopping for new rings.

No, they weren't expensive, fancy rings like my golden wedding band and sparkling engagement ring. They were simple — one silver with a tiny heart, the other a small band of blue and silver entwined.

Nothing extravagant, but oh so meaningful to me. The ring finger on my left hand was still naked, but the two new rings represented love, friendship, and loyalty.

They represented what my heart would learn in time — that things are different now, but that didn't mean my life was over.

That even though I had lost part of my identity, I was still loved, valued, and cherished by God.

That there was still joy and purpose in my life.

And that God would bring so much beauty and joy from the ashes of my heartache.

My friend, there are times when life strips away the identity we cling to. In those times, remember who you are in Jesus. You are the daughter God is proud to call His own, the woman He created to be with Him, the one Jesus gave His very lifeblood to save.

You are loved far beyond what you could ever comprehend. In Psalm 139:17-18, we learn that God's thoughts about us are so many that we could never count them. *How precious also are thy thoughts unto me,*

O God! how great is the sum of them! If I should count them, they are more in number than the sand: when I awake, I am still with thee.

No matter who this world says you are—married, single, divorced, childless, broken, or abandoned—it is who you are in Jesus that matters.

Just as my sweet friend replaced rings of betrayal with rings of love and loyalty, so Jesus takes your old identity and replaces it with what He calls "you," a new creature (2 Corinthians 5:17).

Loved, cherished, and wanted.

| DAY 3 |

Fixed or Fluid
Melody Holloway

I AM THAT I AM. – Exodus 3:14

A few years ago, I heard this explanation about fluid. The structure of fluid allows it to take the shape of whatever it is poured into. Its ability to change is a wonder, but this ability also means that water has no defined shape. It has no shape or identity of it's own. Water is ever changing. It has no will or power to make decisions without being acted upon or influenced by an outside agent. Lastly, water is constantly losing some of itself with each transfer. Wow! I would contend that many of us are often like fluid, like water without a fixed shape or identity. Each new environment means a change in how we present ourselves. Our identities are constantly changing to reflect the values of the "world" we currently belong to. This constant change results in a sense of confusion and anxiety.

The idea of fluidity is appealing. Being free of all labels, stereotypes, defined roles, etc. somewhat resonates with me. Growing up, I had a lot of labels that I ascribed to such as: preacher's kid, Holloway, Christian, black, athlete, smart, etc. While many of these labels were implored in my search for who I really was, I often struggled between having a sense of pride and joy due to these labels and feeling bound and restricted by them. Much of my confusion concerning my identity came from trying to maintain a reputation that would meet the approval of each social circle I encountered. With each label came a new responsibility to be and act a certain way.

This fluidity, the freedom to be whatever we want or feel we should be, has left us in this extremely anxious, confusing, disconcerting, and ultimately degrading situation. Now, as a disclaimer, a confusion of identity is not the sole reason for all that anxiety and stress. However, I do think much of the stress and anxiety that so many experience is due in large part to this question of identity. Anxiety is a response to a stressor. What we believe about ourselves and about God determines how we respond and act. So who are you? Who is God? These are life's most important questions. However, I don't think we have been coming to these questions appropriately.

It's not about who you are, but it is about who God is. We have started with self, but we must start with the Savior. We have put all trust, all focus, all hope in ourselves. We have forgotten God — what He does, what He's done, and who He is. Instead we go on this journey of self-discovery so we can hopefully muster up enough of whatever the world says we need to live this life. As we focus on ourselves, we continually reach the limits of our humanity. I ran across this a couple years ago, and it changed my perspective. In Exodus 3:11-13, we see Moses question who he was and focus on his own power to fulfill His purpose and God's plan.

However, in verse 14, God replied to Moses with, "I AM THAT I AM." Moses did as we do; he started with himself. God, with that simple, yet powerful response, reminded him that it didn't matter whom he was, but that God was the "I AM." "I AM" was all that Moses needed, He is all we need and all that we need to know.

Your identity is not found in a person, a place, a promotion, or a preference. What you do is not who you are, but you are who God says you are; and His voice is the only One with the power to declare anything over your life. I'll close with this. Women are never more valued, uplifted, cared for, and beloved than by the God of the Bible. Any human distortion of God results in a distortion and ultimately destruction of His creation and its intended purpose. Women always lose when Christ is not winning the competition for their body, mind, and soul. Let this encourage you to know your God, know His Word, and know His ways. It is that knowledge that keeps us fixed in a culture that forsakes our Heavenly Father.

Never Change
Alana Brown

Therefore if any man be in Christ, he is a new creature: old things are passed away; behold, all things are become new. -
2 Corinthians 5:17

"Never change," said the devoted friend to the well-beloved confidant.

I have heard it in conversations. I have read it in a note. I have heard friend after friend utter it. It's the phrase that is easy to say, but oh so hard to live, "Never change."

I remember yearning to freeze time a few years back. All of my children could buckle themselves into a vehicle; showers were independent of mom or dad; chores could be done at a decent speed; and there was still a whole lot of innocence in those young faces. It felt pretty fulfilling and "never change" felt like a promising feeling.

The problem is that we do change, and when we utter these words, the expectations we place on one another are crippling. Imagine with me that I really could pull an Elsa and freeze those ages of my children. Where would that leave us or rather them? I am afraid that it would leave them stunted, unable to fulfill the great purpose God created for their ever growing lives. For in our finite, mortal selves, we are incapable of not changing.

At the bare minimum, to be human is to change. And as humans, change is something we naturally reject. It is uncomfortable and emotionally often feels unbearable, yet, from day one our bodies and most of all, our character, is forever morphing into the next phase.

While our natural tendency leans into pushing change away, why don't we choose to embrace the beauty that change can bring?

A child who once said, "Mommy, I wuv you!" covered in dirt handing you a bunch of wildflowers freshly picked, is now seeking your advice saying, "Mom, what do you think I should do about this situation?" Proverbs 15:22 tells us, *Without counsel purposes are disappointed.*

A friend who used to share everything with you (aka "gossip") about someone else has now found her satisfaction in Christ and is striving to become more like Him. She hasn't pulled away or held back; she's grown. Psalm 34:13 tells us, *Keep thy tongue from evil, and thy lips from speaking guile.*

A body that once stood strong but now is stricken with disease is not broken but is made whole in its weakness by the power of its Savior. 2 Corinthians 12:9 tells us, *My grace is sufficient for thee: for my strength is made perfect in weakness. Most gladly therefore will I rather glory in my infirmities, that the power of Christ may rest upon me.*

A church that stands firm on the doctrine of Scripture yet is willing to engage and be on the front lines of their culture in order to share the gospel hasn't thrown in the towel; they are in the battle. 1 Corinthians 9:22 tells us, *To the weak became I as weak, that I might gain the weak: I am made all things to all men, that I might by all means save some.*

A region that has grown with people is not an annoyance but an opportunity to touch more lives for Jesus. 2 Peter 3:9 tells us, *The Lord is not slack concerning his promise, as some men count slackness; but is longsuffering to us-ward, not willing that any should perish, but that all should come to repentance.*

The list of changes in life is endless, but we serve the One who is boundless. And with that, I hope I am changing. I hope you are changing. I pray that I am not the same woman I was yesterday, for if I am, I'm missing something.

The God who saved and redeemed my life did not sacrifice so much for me to sit idly by and "Never Change." He's working. He's moving. He's molding. Instead of rejecting this change, let's embrace it!

And while, HE NEVER CHANGES, you can be assured that He wants a great change in you.

Check Yourself Before You Wreck Yourself
Tamara Weatherbee

Thou art worthy, O Lord, to receive glory and honour and power: for thou hast created all things, and for thy pleasure they are and were created. - Revelation 4:11

To the woman who lost her identity, let's talk about some much needed biblical truths. No fluff. No filters. Just the good stuff.

If you don't know me, Hi! I'm Tamara, a stay-at-home mom with three kids and I absolutely love it! I am also what the younger generation would call a "Social Media Influencer."

Blah!

I hate that term. But hey, it pays the bills! (Disney bills still count, right?) My life is pretty much out there for the world (or just my followers) to see, and sometimes I get backlash and even hate messages. Whether they stem from judgement, jealousy, or just plain boredom I don't know, but some of them are HARSH!

Thankfully, I can now honestly say they don't bother me in the least. When I first started my social media journey I did get some comments and concern from friends and family. "Are you putting too much out there?"... "What if so and so sees this?"... "I can't believe you looked like that live on Facebook."

So I thought to myself, as a Christian who serves in ministry along side my husband who is an assistant pastor, I never want to give my church, my pastor, my family, or God a bad name, or paint them in a bad light. I think I had one of those "come to Jesus" moments.

These are some questions I asked myself.
- Is my identity on social media true to who I am in the privacy of my home?
- Do I need to hide certain parts of my life thinking people might judge me?
- Is my identity based on being perfect? (spoiler alert, never gonna happen).
- Do I seek praise or approval from others as my source of worth?
- Does the way I live my life line up with the life God has for me?
- If my life points in the direction of Christ, should I even give two hoots about other opinions? (I have no idea what two hoots means. My mom just often said it).

This come to Jesus moment caused me to get out of my anxiety and fear of what others thought about me and solely focus on God.

You see, Jesus understood what it was like to be judged. He knew what it was like to be praised one day and mocked the next. People talked about him telling others who they thought He was and what He should do. But He remained faithful because His identity was not in their opinion- it was in His Father.

Isn't it crazy to know that Jesus was perfect and yet He was still made fun of, judged, mocked, and even crucified? This is awesome and so comforting y'all!! Because we know there is no level of achievement we could ever reach that would give us the approval of every woman or man.

Let me say it louder for the people in the back... WE ARE NOT HERE FOR THE APPROVAL OF OTHERS! The ultimate opinion that should matter to us is God's! To live off the approval of Christ alone frees me to love others with no hidden agenda. I am not seeking anything from them in return.

Do you know why you were created? Sounds silly and basic I know, but think about it.

Why were YOU created?

Revelation 4:11 says, *Thou art worthy, O Lord, to receive glory and honour and power: for thou hast created all things, and for thy pleasure they are and were created.*

We were created to bring honor and glory to the Lord! THAT'S IT. If we focus on that, everything else should just fall into place, right? So lets focus on the next step.

Knowing that, how do we find our identity in Christ? Starting back in the Garden of Eden to the time of "Little house on the Prairie" to even now Jesus is still the same?

Hebrews 13:8 says, *Jesus Christ, the same yesterday, and to day and for ever.* This also means His Word never changes about you. Check out these verses and how Jesus describes us.

"Children of Light" Ephesians 5:8
"Fearfully and wonderfully made" Psalm 139:14
"More precious than rubies" Proverbs 3:15

He made you unique, specifically to carry out His purpose. We are set apart to live a life glorifying Him (Jeremiah 1:5). With God's Word as your roadmap and anchor, you can live freely knowing you are who God says you are.

Oftentimes, we are so busy trying to please others that we miss our true purpose and the joy that comes from living out our identity in Christ.

So let's live bravely and boldly for HIM. "Check yourself before you wreck yourself." It's corny I know, but ask yourself this before you make decisions: "Is what I'm doing, saying, watching, etc. honoring and pleasing to the Lord?"

Once you find your identity in Christ you can begin living in the joy of the Lord. Not worried about what others think or say because God is our ultimate judge. Trust me there will always be haters, friends, or other women secretly judging you (maybe some not so secretly). Give it to God. Live peacefully and joyfully knowing your identity is found in Him and in Him alone.

Week Two

| DAY 6 |

What's in a Name?
Jennifer Selver

But ye are a chosen generation, a royal priesthood, an holy nation, a peculiar people; that ye should shew forth the praises of him who hath called you out of darkness into his marvellous light. - 1 Peter 2:9

Before I was married my last name was Smart. So, yes, you guessed it. I was the subject of a lot of jokes. It was assumed by many that I would get the best grades. It was assumed that I knew all the answers. It was assumed that I was the "smart" one in the class. Although this wasn't always the case, my last name became my identity. My sister and I were known as "The Smart Girls." We often heard, "Ohhhhh, you're Dr. Smart's daughters!" I couldn't hide from that last name. My identity was wrapped up in my name.

identity
i ·den ·ti ·ty
noun - the fact of being who or what a person or thing is (Oxford)

What name are you identified with? Do you know who you really are? Are you hiding behind someone else's expectation? Are you your real self in your relationships? Do you seek to identify with words like "sexy," "cool," or "popular?"

Many of us struggle with our true identity because of external pressures. Some call them stressors. These stressors come from comparison to other girls; the pictures that we see in books or magazines; and, of course, on social media and the many influencers connected to it. The messages out there tell us what pretty is supposed to look like; what brave is supposed to look like; and what love is supposed to look like. And if we do or don't do certain things, then we can be identified with a particular group or class of people. The pretty ones, the brave ones, the loved ones.

But, do you know Whose opinion is the only opinion that really matters? Do you know Who has The Truth to everything we need to know about ourselves? The One Who created us, Our Father in Heaven. He gave us His Word that tells us the truth about who we are. Our Father God has already identified us with many names found in His Word. If you have been adopted into His family, you can guarantee that He has already given you a royal identity that cannot be changed or taken away.

Here are just a few of the names that God calls us:

Beloved Child of God
Beloved, now are we the sons (and daughters) of God, and it doth not yet appear what we shall be: but we know that, when he shall appear, we shall be like him; for we shall see him as he is. - 1 John 3:2 (emphasis added)

Friend
I call you not servants; for the servant knoweth not what his lord doeth: but I have called you friends; for all things

*that I have heard of my Father I have made known unto
you.* - John 15:15

His Masterpiece
*For we are his workmanship (masterpiece), created in
Christ Jesus unto good works, which God hath before
ordained that we should walk in them.* - Ephesians 2:10
(emphasis added)

Daughter
*And will be a Father unto you, and ye shall be my sons and
daughters, saith the Lord Almighty.* - 2 Corinthians 6:18

Accepted
*To the praise of the glory of his grace, wherein he hath made
us accepted in the beloved.* - Ephesians 1:6

I have only listed a few of the many names God calls
His children throughout Scripture.
What new name do you need to claim as your true
identity?

Are you struggling with self-worth, then claim the
name, "Masterpiece."

Are you struggling with love from others, then claim
the name, "Beloved."

Are you struggling with fatherlessness, then claim the
name, "Daughter of God."

Are you struggling with feeling left out, then claim
the name, "Accepted."

The beautiful thing is you don't have to settle for just one name, you can claim them all and more! The truth of Scripture will apply to your life today, tomorrow, and forever!

Bible Study Challenge: Study the Word of God and discover the names that God has crafted personally for you. Meditate on His promises found in these names and claim these truths as your own.

Escaping the "I" Zone
Amanda Thorne

Look not every man on his own things, but every man also on the things of others. – Philippians 2:4

I let out a sigh of relief as I turn the kitchen faucet off, start the dishwasher, dry off my hands, and hang up the kitchen towel. Then I hear a clink! I turn to see that my son has dropped his dirty plate and fork in my clean sink. Another one is right behind him and my husband follows suit. Within five minutes of conquering the dirty dishes, the sink is again full and more dirty dishes are ready to be washed.

I punch the air in victory as I close the dresser drawer in my boy's room. The laundry is done! I turn to leave, and there in the corner lies yesterday's discarded togs. I sigh as I pick them up and toss them in the empty laundry hamper.

I stretch my arms happily after I put the bucket and mop away and smile proudly at my clean floors. Then I hear an "Oops!" I turn around to see a puddle of spilled, sticky red fruit punch on my otherwise clean floor and the sheepish grin of my four year old. Exhausted, I grab the bucket and mop and begin again.

Never Ending, Mundane, Exhausting ... these could all describe the scenarios above, and if I am not careful I can dwell on the negative aspects of these jobs. It feels like no matter what I do, it never makes a difference. Your day may look different from mine, but you may find that you describe it the same way — a series of repeated, never ending thankless tasks!

How do we escape the negative outlook? It's so easy to grumble and complain. It's no wonder that all through the Old Testament we see God get so aggravated with the children of Israel, and then we step over to the New Testament and we are told over and over to give thanks and do all things without grumbling. Do you want to know what keeps me in the negative state of mind? It is pride. "I" am always having to do the dishes. "I" am always doing laundry. "I" am always cleaning up after my kids.

When I'm in the "I" zone, I will always be frustrated, grumbly, and unthankful. The "I" zone is a very miserable place. It is a deep dark pit, and it will swallow you whole if you don't watch out. It will steal your joy in an instant. You will flip out at your husband for putting that fork in the sink. You will leave your desk job with a very sour attitude. You will lose sight of the call God has put on your life. It is time to step away from pride and escape the "I" zone.

Our culture is constantly telling us to do things for ourselves. "Do it for you" is plastered on billboards and in magazines. It's the mantra of every social media platform. "Me Time," "Focusing on Me," "A Better Me," all of these are presented in such a subtle and harmless way, but the reality is they ooze with pride.

This is one way Satan works against us. He takes subtle things and draws us in. With these little "harmless" phrases he has caused us to take our eyes off Jesus and put them on ourselves. *"Love one another." "Look not every man on his own things but every man also on the things of others." "Be ye kind one to another" "In everything give thanks." "Think on things that are true, honest, just, pure, lovely."* A life focused on Jesus will have these phrases at the forefront of our minds and actions.

Let's look back at my day. When I step out of the "I" zone and put my focus on Christ my perspective changes. I may get frustrated at first that my kitchen sink and laundry hampers are never empty, but I can stop myself and give thanks that I have a family to serve and take care of.

I may get agitated at my child for spilling his drink on my freshly mopped floor, but when I am focused on Jesus I can quickly redirect my thoughts and emotions.

This lifestyle is a choice, and it takes work; but this lifestyle is a profitable one. You will have less strife and more joy. You will find that negativity will start to disappear, and you will surround yourself with those who have the same focus. Will things always go right? Of course not! But you will be able to face them with a different mindset, and that will make all the difference.

| DAY 8 |

Asking God Why
Lysandra Osterkamp

Now there are diversities of gifts, but the same Spirit. And there are differences of administrations, but the same Lord. And there are diversities of operations, but it is the same God which worketh all in all. For as the body is one, and hath many members, and all the members of that one body, being many, are one body: so also is Christ. - 1 Corinthians 12:4-5, 12

"Why can't I do this? Why is this so hard?" I threw my hands up in the air giving up. I can't, I don't have the ability. Why? Why didn't God allow me to have this ability? I'm trying my very best, I'm putting the work into it. I have the heart to do it, I even have the right motives. So why? Why can't I?

When I was seventeen, I knew I was going to marry a pastor. My soon to be husband was in seminary and he let me know that, as a pastor's wife, it would be helpful if I could play the piano. I was on board immediately. Almost every pastor's wife I knew played the piano and it was an incredibly useful skill.

In my senior year of high school, I set out to learn how to play the piano. I bought a keyboard, sheet music, and hired a teacher. I tried so hard. I practiced day and night. I failed. No matter what I did or how much I practiced, I couldn't play the piano well.

I didn't understand. I was even praying for God to give me this gift. I was asking for a gift so I could use it for Him. Why? Why wouldn't He say yes and make me a piano player? I knew He had the power to make me anything He wanted. Yes, I believe the God who did miracles in the Bible is the God of today. The harder I tried, the more I realized it would take a real miracle for me to play the piano.

God was not giving me this ability. I had to let it go. I had to accept that I would be a "pianoless" pastor's wife. I felt like such a disappointment, to God, to my husband, and to my church. Until I asked God "Why." I asked, "Why didn't you allow me to play the piano for you, God? What's your plan for me?"

It was a huge relief when God answered my prayer. In my heart, I felt Him say. "That's not what I want from you. You can let that go. I have other plans for you based on the gifts I have already given you. Use those for me."

Once I realized this truth, I did let the piano dream die and focused on that with which God had already gifted me. I began to have a new excitement over the things I COULD do rather than dwell on that which I couldn't do. I dove in. I went all-in for Jesus using the talents I had, even if they weren't my first choice. Don't be disappointed with how God made you. You have gifts, abilities, and talents right now. Use those for God. Don't wish you had someone else's gift. Don't be like me and think the only way to serve God is in one particular way. Look for the ways He has already gifted you and use what you already have for Him.

If there is that thing you wish you could do or you wish you could be, don't be afraid to humbly ask God "Why?" He has an answer for you.

God purposefully made you the way you are. God did not make a mistake when He made you. God did not give you the wrong gifts. He made you for a purpose. Give Him your all, then you will find beautiful joy!

I will praise thee; for I am fearfully and wonderfully made: marvellous are thy works; and that my soul knoweth right well. - Psalm 139:14

The Identity Crisis
Sharon Rabon

Therefore if any man be in Christ, he is a new creature: old things are passed away; behold, all things are become new. - 2 Corinthians 5:17

I am the wife of Tim Rabon, the mom of Tim, Philip and Joy, the "mom" of Laura, Nichole and Chris and I'm known as Nana to eight Cute Kids. My church family calls me the Pastor's wife and my office door says that I'm the Pastor's Secretary. I think of myself as a counselor, mentor, leader of ladies, and a friend. I identify with being a decorator, wedding director, organizer, and speaker.

Some of these titles are who I am and some of them are what I do. Can you identify the difference? Who am I? Do I have an identity crisis?

Our sense of identity is often tied up in what we do and not who we are. Our priorities conflict but our identity should never conflict with who we are or what we do. I am not just sometimes Nana, I am always Nana to my Cute Kids. I am not just occasionally Mom to my kids. I'm always proud to answer when they call. I'm not just the wife of Tim Rabon when I feel good. I'm always thankful and proud to be his wife.

Wearing many hats causes us to confuse our priorities with whom we really are. It has been said that a woman actually becomes three different women over the course of her life. I think I might be on that third person. I change due to age and responsibility, but my identity is the same.

Answer these questions to help you identify who you are so that you can better prioritize what you do.

1. Am I a child of God? My life must revolve around my identity as a Christian. God is not pleased when I misrepresent Him. 2 Corinthians 5:17 assures us, *Therefore if any man be in Christ, he is a new creature: old things are passed away; behold, all things are become new.* Are you a child of God?

2. What does God expect of me? God gave me a 7-day week with 24 hours in each day. He does not expect me to fit more into my day than will fit. God gave us one day per week to rest. He set up the day and night for a purpose. God expects me to serve Him diligently and give Him my best. Are you doing what God expects of you?

3. How do I prioritize my identities? First, I'm a wife, then a mom. Nana comes next. We have a responsibility to come alongside of our children to pray for and spiritually guide them. The roles of Pastor's wife and friend follow suit. Roles will vary for us according to the time of life or our career choices. Roles change but who I am within those roles should never change. How do you prioritize your identities?

4. Do I choose to please Christ or please others?

Pleasing others often crowds out what we should do because we do not want to disappoint those we want to please. Galatians 1:10 warns us, *For do I now persuade men, or God? or do I seek to please men? for if I yet pleased men, I should not be the servant of Christ.* Whom do you choose to please?

5. What changes do I need to make in order to overcome my identity crisis? I don't want to be someone who runs here and there accomplishing nothing. I want to see changes that need to be made and make those changes in a timely manner. My desire is to please God; therefore, I must identify with Him and prioritize accordingly.

Consider Galatians 2:20: *I am crucified with Christ: nevertheless I live, yet not I, but Christ liveth in me: and the life which I now live in the flesh I live by the faith of the Son of God, who loved me, and gave himself for me.* What changes do you need to make?

List "who you are" in order of priority. Make an effort to live in order as those relationships are prioritized. List what you do. Prioritize this list, too. If some of these titles need to be dropped in order to better be who you are, then do so.

Ask yourself, "Do I have an identity crisis?"

Did Someone Steal Your ID?
Stephanie Willard

The thief cometh not, but for to steal, and to kill, and to destroy: I am come that they might have life, and that they might have it more abundantly. - John 10:10

We all have those moments of panic...

We rush back to the store, looking for the misplaced wallet, only to go home without it, wondering who has it and how quickly we can cancel all our credit cards and notify the bank.

Or we may get a notification from our bank via email or text that an unusual charge was just made in our name. What do we do?

We fear the worst.
We freeze up.
And if we're not quick to be proactive, we lose our identity to a thief. This loss could potentially cost us TONS of money and grief.

It happens every day in our world but how often do we allow it to happen in our walk with Jesus?

As a believer in Christ, we are redeemed, chosen, called by God to fulfill His purpose for our lives and transformed by the Gospel to be changed into His image, and point others to the transforming power of the Gospel.

But the Enemy knows He can't steal us out of our Father's Hand (John 10:28-29) when we have trusted Jesus for our eternal salvation. So, he tries the next best thing: he deceives us into believing that someone else's view of who we are is MORE IMPORTANT than God's view of who we REALLY are.

Here's what that may look like:

- We live in FEAR of what other people may think or say about us.

- We hide from opportunities that require social interaction.

- We lack the courage to use our voices for good, fearing rejection, judgment, criticism, or misunderstanding.

- We replay in our minds and hearts the hurtful words that have been spoken to us or about us.

- We struggle to see ourselves the way our loving and compassionate Heavenly Father sees us, and choose others' views of ourselves over His view.

Once the Enemy has attacked our identity, he has us right where he wants us: afraid and ashamed of who we are; afraid and ashamed to attempt great things for the Kingdom.

But there is always HOPE in the Gospel, friend!!!

We can REPLACE the twisted and deceived view of our identity by RECLAIMING the courage and confidence found in these steps to victory:

- **REPLACE** our fear of man with fear of/faith in God. (Proverbs 29:25)

- **RESIST** the temptation to be a VICTIM and choose to be a VICTOR. (Romans 8:37)

- **RESET** some healthy relationship boundaries — social media, friendships, acquaintances, etc. (Hebrews 10:24)

- **REJECT** the lies you've believed about yourself and replaces them with the TRUTH of God's Word. (Philippians 4:8)

- **REST** in the knowledge of His love for you, and His willingness to fight your battles FOR you and WITH you. (Jeremiah 33:3; 2 Chronicles 20:15; and Jude 1:24)

- **RENEW** your purpose for living/loving the abundant life God wants you to experience DAILY! (John 10:10)

Week Three

ENCOURAGEMENT FROM WOMEN

Vellus Hair
Shelley Conway

And many of the Samaritans of that city believed on him for the saying of the woman, which testified, He told me all that ever I did. - John 4:39

It took 6 years! The first time I heard "cancer" was back in 2013 — 8 years ago. Exactly three weeks into my chemotherapy regime I lost ALL my hair... every single strand, including my nose hairs that kept the sniffles from running and dropping freely whenever and wherever they wanted. I know... too much information, right?

I was shocked when I went bald. People I had known for years seemed almost afraid to look at me, unsure of what to say and not wanting to stare at a sight that neither of us had seen before. Just as I and everyone else noticed my bare scalp, neither I nor anyone else noticed all the other little hairs that vanished as well, including those, pale, peach-fuzz-like hairs all over my face. They are called Vellus Hair and, believe it or not, they have a role to play. It took 6 years for my little vellus hairs to finally come back in on my face (the eyebrows and eyelashes are still lacking but that's a separate conversation!).

The vellus hairs are actually important, even though you don't really pay much attention to them. They help regulate the body's temperature. Sweat wets the hair, as the wetness comes to the end of the hair it evaporates, and the process continues. They are designed to cool the body, or help retain heat when it's cold. During my cancer treatments my body couldn't handle cold or hot temperatures. Obviously, there were a LOT of factors that came into play when it came to the reasons as to why my body struggled with temperature control, but those little tiny hairs played a part, no matter how small.

All of these qualities about our bodies work together in a truly miraculous way. Does life go on without one or two of those "little things" working properly? Yes. But, perhaps, not quite as smoothly. When you remove a little thing called an appendix, life changes but continues. Same thing with a gall bladder or tonsils. However, if all of those bodily systems are working properly, as the Lord designed them, life can be so much easier!

I'm a vellus hair.

People don't really notice if I'm missing or not. The party and fellowship go on without me. Meetings and conferences don't come to a grinding halt if I'm not there; the speaker and crowd continue on, not missing a beat. Church continues without me. Ministry continues without me. The office runs without me, etc., etc., etc.

You and I might be alike in that matter! But I want you to sit back and listen to me for just one more minute...

God uses even a little vellus hair. Why did God put

those little hairs all over my face? I mean, really, a lot of women spend quite a bit of time and effort to remove them!

God designed our bodies in a truly miraculous, breathtaking way that most of us cannot begin to understand. It takes many years of schooling to begin comprehending even just one portion of our complex body. Older bodies are different than younger bodies. Some bodies have allergies, some have different melanin, chromosomes, eye color, height, etc. We are very complicated beings! Yet on most everyone you'll find those little vellus hairs.

Now, let's take a look at our roles in life. Whether we admit to it or not, oftentimes a person's "value" to a community is based on her importance as seen with our insignificant human mindset. But, ladies, I am here to tell you that you don't have to have a degree in theology, or even be a Pastor's or Deacon's wife.

You don't have to be in charge of the office, run a company, be on a board of directors, be on the front lines of healthcare, have a sizable income, be married or single, have no children or twelve, etc., to be important to God OR — wait for it — to be USED by God.

There are so many instances in the Bible where God uses an unlikely person. In fact, many of us would venture to say that in some instances God has used what we may consider to be an "unsuitable" person. Consider the Samaritan woman. After she spoke with Jesus at the well, she returned to her town and told the denizens about Jesus. The result? An entire town come out to see Jesus and over the next two days many were saved and began following Christ!

One woman.

One woman who listened, got excited about what Jesus said, and went back to her town and told everyone around her what she had learned. God used one woman to reach *many of the Samaritans of that city.* John 4:39

Our world desperately needs revival. So many people who need a Savior. We continue to pray that our churches will reopen and that the Lord will allow pastors to again fill the pulpits as the Covid scare subsides. But, in my humble opinion, we can't wait for pastors to be heard, or churches to grow, or evangelists to draw large crowds. It has to start with us. It has to start in our own hearts. Just like our bodies need those little hairs to accomplish a much larger objective, God uses one heart to impact hundreds. "HUNDREDS?! Hundreds, you say?! Nope, not me! I don't have that kind of an impact!! Why, we only have 65 members in our church!"

Sociologists tell us that the most introverted of people will influence 10,000 others in an average lifetime. (Online Forbes, What is Your Impact, Erin Urban). Imagine, just imagine, how many people you have knowingly and unknowingly influenced in your life so far! You are only one person. That's true. But just as God used the Samaritan woman, and just as God uses the vellus hair, both in very obviously different ways, He uses both to bring about His design and greater purpose.

I may only be but one insignificant little vellus hair when someone else looks at the overall picture, but I want God to see me and my heart. I want Him to see a softhearted and obedient servant that is willing to fulfill whatever small role He might give me, to accomplish an objective that no human eye or mind can behold.

Now... read 1 Corinthians 12:14-31.

| DAY 12 |

When I Don't Feel Loved
Jen Holmes

As the Father hath loved me, so have I loved you: continue ye in my love. These things have I spoken unto you, that my joy might remain in you, and that your joy might be full. - John 15:9, 11

They say that deep down, everyone is asking the same few questions, one of those being, Am I really loved?

The Bible is full of verses telling us that we are loved by God. We can read it over and over in the Psalms, in the Gospels, even the most famous verse in the Bible is all about how God so loved the whole world that He gave His Son for us. A quick Google search can bring up one hundred verses to remind us of God's love.

So why is it so hard to feel loved?

Why do we wonder if we're the one that God must have given up on? Or the one that needs to earn His love because we're not good enough? Why do we strive and worry and cry?

Because we're listening to how we feel.

For some reason we often feel unloved. It could be a driven personality, something in our past, spiritual attack, depression, difficult circumstances — the why doesn't matter as much as the fact that we find ourselves feeling alone and unloved. And that's okay. You're allowed to feel how you feel. Emotions are not bad.

They're just not always true.

Jesus is teaching us here in these verses in John how to feel loved. These verses come right in the passage about abiding in Him. Earlier He said, *I am the vine, ye are the branches: He that abideth in me, and I in him, the same bringeth forth much fruit: for without me ye can do nothing.*

He then goes on to talk about how we are loved. And that He wants us to know we are loved so that our joy might be full.

Jesus understands that we need to be reassured of His love over and over and knowing that we are loved is essential to our joy. The way we feel loved is to abide in Him. Because without Him, we can do nothing!

I find it so interesting that these two ideas are in the same passage. Jesus wants us to feel loved so that our joy will be full, and also reminds us that we can do nothing without Him. Our emotions are powerful things, often too powerful for us to handle on our own, and yet we must always be analyzing them to see if they are telling us the truth. When they're not, we must subject them to the truth of Scripture.

The truth is, you are loved. Fully and completely by the Creator of the universe and there is nothing else you need to do that could make Him love you more. The truth is that you can find joy in that fact, you can choose to believe it and rest in His love, no matter what your emotions tell you.

But you can't do it alone.

You need to abide in Jesus to turn those emotions around. Read about his love. Memorize the passages that tell you about it. Remind yourself of His sacrifice for you. Have honest conversations with God about how you feel. Let Him remind you of the truth.

Abide in Him and you will start to believe the truth and your joy will be full.

God Is Love!
Grace Hayes

Beloved, let us love one another: for love is of God; and every one that loveth is born of God, and knoweth God. He that loveth not knoweth not God; for God is love. - 1 John 4:7-8

As a five year old, I was repeatedly taken out to our shed by a man in our church and sexually abused. Without even realizing it, this formed my identity. I was insecure, feeling alone — never feeling protected or safe. I felt insignificant and compared myself to others paradoxically, both to feel superior as well as to remind myself of my inadequacies. I sought the approval of others because it made me feel loved and accepted. I viewed everything negative (and sometimes even the positive) through the lens of being unprotected, unsafe, unloved, insignificant, and always alone. This skewed identity became my prison. My chains. I began to feel as if I were in a loop — a never ending cycle of despair.

Now, please. Don't feel sorry for me. God has broken these chains through the power of the gospel through the work of Jesus on the cross, His Word/Truth, and the help of an amazing therapist. I have learned what it means to be freed from an identity imposed upon me from past traumas, experiences, and people. So girl, can I just share who I am because of Christ? Maybe you need to be reminded of who you are in Him as well. I am accepted. Yep. Just the way I am.

With all of my awesomeness and all of my flaws. He doesn't roll His eyes at my mistakes, shrug His shoulders in disappointment, and turn away. Nope. I am eternally loved and accepted.

Can we just all admit that we can be VERY unlovable? And yet because of Who He is, He never stops loving us. He puts no conditions on His love. In fact, it is His love that continually draws me to Him. I am safe. As a hen protects her chicks, He hides me under His wings. When the crazy comes my way, He allows it, not to harm me, but because He loves me. You see, the crazy is what He uses to gently bring my focus back to Him. The crazy allows me to get rid of those things that bear me down and hold me back from living out my life for His glory. But even through the crazy … I am still safe, completely protected in His arms. I am significant. He knows me. He sees me. He actively listens to me. I am unique. I am so thankful for what He has allowed in my life. All the good. All the bad. All of it.

You see, I am who I am because of Who He is and my life experiences. Pretty cool right? So why compare? I have strengths and weaknesses. So do you. I have life experiences that have molded me. So do you. Is that not beautiful? I don't need to feel lesser than or greater than you. I can appreciate your uniqueness and celebrate it as I do my own. I am never alone. Being in ministry can "feel" very lonely and living in a foreign culture seems to magnify this feeling. And yet, He is always there. His presence dwells within me. I have access to His comfort, His counsel, His support, His guidance, and His power. So when the feelings of loneliness creep in, I just take a deep breath and thank Him for never ever leaving me alone. I am His daughter! A child of the King! This is my identity. This is who I am.

From Prostitute to Princess
Kelly Edmondson

For the LORD your God, he is God in heaven above, and in earth beneath. - Joshua 2:11

I met Allison in college. We played soccer together — her tiny frame and feisty spirit directly behind my long legs and calm demeanor. To be frank, I kept her out of fights. Allison spent time as a child of missionaries in the Dominican Republic. After graduation she returned to the island, married a preacher, started a church, a school, and a safe house for prostitutes. It was on the island that we met again, working side-by-side in the streets of San Pedro, some 15 years after graduation.

"The women come out at dusk," she told me. "Most of them were trafficked into the sex trade between the ages of eleven and fourteen. I will introduce you tonight. Bring the doctor. We will host a small, private clinic at the church tomorrow."

We strolled the streets as the sun sank low in the Caribbean sky. The doctor, Allison, and I meandered past the street vendors selling food, the cantinas selling drinks, and toward the intersection where the sex workers stood … selling themselves. The women smiled as we approached. Allison knew them well. They embraced and kissed her as she called each by name and introduced us.

The doctor told them about the clinic to be held at the church the next day. I half listened as I looked at my feet awkwardly, and watched beetles crawl across a discarded styrofoam cup on the ground. What does one say to women who sell themselves for money? What does one discuss on a street corner at dusk while the pimps and boyfriends watch from the shadows?

I lifted my head and looked one woman in the face. "Do you have children?" I asked.

"I do," she replied with a smile. "I work to care for them." She reached into her pocket and pulled out a cell phone, scrolled through pictures and showed me a photo of her four smiling children.

"I have four as well," I responded. "Please bring your children to the clinic tomorrow. We have vitamins."

By now, Allison urged us on to the next location. She nodded toward the shadows. "The men will be angered if we hinder their women from work." We headed off into the night to find more lost sheep.

The clinic went well the next day. Several women came and brought their children. We were busy with exams and tests and educating and handing out prescriptions. We treated each woman with dignity. Allison shared Christ with those who had never heard. She told them about the church and her workshop which provides discipleship and education to learn the art of making jewelry and clothing. We left happy and humbled to practice medicine with such needy patients.

That night, in the safety of my room with my husband, I began to think of Rahab in Joshua, chapter 2. That prostitute boldly looked the Hebrew spies in the face and confessed, "I believe in your God and I need you to save me and my family."

Many Christian women can identify with Rahab—the cleaned up version, at least. Rahab is listed in Hebrews as a woman of faith (Heb. 11:31). She is named in Matthew as part of Christ's genealogy (Matt. 1:5). She was daring and hopeful as she slung the scarlet rope out of her window as the spies raced away into the distance. What we find hard to accept is that Rahab was a sex worker. She lived on the outer wall where according to historical texts the poor and disreputable lived. She was uneducated, most likely fraught with sexually transmitted infections, coarse, and bawdy. It's no wonder that she spoke so boldly to the spies—she was used to working with men. She no doubt had been slapped around, abused, disrespected, and eventually discarded. What did she have to lose?

It's hard for me to reconcile the two Rahabs—the prostitute versus the princess. One selling herself to survive, the other standing beside her prince husband watching her son marry Ruth. The difference between Rahab before and after is complex and yet, pretty simple. The difference is Jesus. When Rahab chose to join the Hebrews it was simply because she believed in their God. She eventually learned of the coming Messiah and became the great-great-so-many-great grandmother of Jesus Christ Himself!

The business of Jesus changing lives is still in operation. There are still prostitutes who can become princesses. Not literally, of course, but daughters of the King. Followers of Jesus. My friend Allison knows this. Her feisty spirit on the soccer field is now revealing itself on the streets of the Dominican Republic. May we, like Allison, strive to reach those princesses while we can.

| DAY 15 |

A Few Good Women
Joanna Alipalo

For thou hast possessed my reins: thou hast covered me in my mother's womb I will praise thee; for I am fearfully and wonderfully made: marvellous are thy works; and that my soul knoweth right well. - Psalm 139:13-14

I was at a friend's house, the television was on, and a question came up in one of the game shows, "Where do we need a few good women?"

To which a contestant answered, "strippers."

Another guy was called on, completely unaware of what the other contestant had answered, and he too answered, "strippers."

I was flabbergasted. Are they being serious? That's the best they could come up with?

Few good women = strippers?

Ladies, how heartbreaking is this? How ridiculous it is that PERHAPS many in today's society think that women are mostly good or only good in doing such a thing?

The Bible says in Psalm 139:13-14, *For thou hast possessed my reins: thou hast covered me in my mother's womb. I will praise thee; for I am fearfully and wonderfully made: marvellous are thy works; and that my soul knoweth right well.*

Ladies, we are more than just objects. We are more than just entertainers. We are more than just man pleasers. God has created us, intricately and lovingly, after His own image and has a purpose for us if we surrender our lives to Him: a purpose that is better than all our dreams and tasks that are not superficial, but make an impact for eternity.

So to answer the question, "Where do we need a few good women?"

We need them at home to care and love family members. We need them at school to patiently teach and help others. We need them at the workplace to work with integrity and to the best of their abilities. We need them at church to serve and pray for the body of Christ and those that are lost. We need them in the streets, all over the world, to share the truth about Christ and to be an extension of His ministry.

Ladies, that's our purpose. That's where we belong. We need a few good women (in fact, we need many!) in every corner of the earth living to glorify our Savior!

And IF there is someone reading this that has a broken past, things about you that you will never have the courage to share with another soul, or maybe someone who is in the sex trade right now, know that Jesus LOVES you deeply. Your story does not have to end here. He is THE answer. He is our only hope.

1 John 4:10 gives us the bottom line, *Herein is love, not that we loved God, but that he loved us, and sent his Son to be the propitiation for our sins.*

Week Four

ENCOURAGEMENT FROM WOMEN

| DAY 16 |

Mended Again
Faith York

He healeth the broken in heart, and bindeth up their wounds. - Psalms 147:3

I intended to use my daughter's curtains as a decoration for a wedding. She brought them to me early that morning and asked if I'd hang them for her. I told her I would do it later that evening. Unfortunately she got impatient and tried to do it herself. She tore the curtain rod out of the wall accidentally. So she decided to enlist her older brother's help.

All of the sudden, I heard something fall over, then crying, yelling, chaos. When I got to her bedroom I found her crying hysterically because the stool to her vanity was broken. Her brother had used it to step on to reach the curtain rod. Only it broke and he fell. She was upset about the stool and he was upset that she wasn't upset because he had fallen. The curtains lay in disarray on the floor.

I made sure everyone was okay and then hung the curtains. I told her to put all the broken pieces of the stool in a pile and daddy would fix them. But that wasn't good enough. She followed me around the house, still crying. We got to the laundry room and I asked her, "Has there ever been something daddy couldn't fix? No. He won't be mad, he'll just fix it for you. So stop crying and worrying about it, it's going to be okay."

As I'm loading clothes into the dryer, the Lord whispers to my heart, "Are you listening to what you just said? As your Daddy, Abba, is there anything I can't fix?"

I'm so tired of feeling broken. Unfixable. Beyond repair. See, my daughter didn't wait on me. And she messed up. And instead of focusing on her brother, who was only trying to help, she just saw what was broken.

She had gotten that vanity for her birthday and had sat on that stool day after day. Playing dress up, makeup, doing her school work. It was precious to her. And in that moment, she only saw the broken leg, the shattered wood. In her eyes, beyond repair. Not good for anything now. She wasn't thinking about her daddy. The one who can fix anything.

I have confidence in her daddy, too. Because I've seen him work on things until they are fixed. The stool will show signs of being broken. It might be a little more fragile after it's fixed. But it can still be used. It will still have a purpose.

And if worse comes to worst and he can't fix it, he loves the little girl who bawled her eyes out because of her precious, broken stool. He'll get her a new one. And it might be even better than the last.

Why don't I have more confidence in *my Father*? I've seen Him work miracles. He reached into the depths of sin to rescue me, so why would I think my brokenness now would be too hard for Him to fix? Why is my focus on the shattered pieces of my life rather than my Savior?

Yes, I've watched some of my precious dreams slip through my hands. My hopes, wishes ... I know He can fix this. And if He chooses not to, whatever He does instead will still have purpose. I may always carry the marks of being put back together. But then again, He may give me something new, better, and more beautiful than what I was before.

If you're worrying about the broken pieces you've put in a pile, waiting and wondering if God can fix them—just stop. It's going to be okay. He can fix it and if He doesn't, He's working on something else for you. You might not look the same when He's done, but you'll be mended once again.

Remain
Mindy Flanagan

Abide in me, and I in you. As the branch cannot bear fruit of itself, except it abide in the vine; no more can ye, except ye abide in me. I am the vine, ye are the branches: He that abideth in me, and I in him, the same bringeth forth much fruit: for without me ye can do nothing. - John 15:4-5

As Christians, we often hear the term "abide or remain," but what exactly does that mean? It is described as something that remains where it is; to continue in a fixed state or endure. In this context, it is referring to maintaining an unbroken communion with Jesus.

In this passage, God uses the branch and the vine to show His relationship to His people. A branch depends on the vine for sustenance to live, grow, and produce fruit. Just as a branch cannot bear fruit unless it is connected to the vine, we, as believers, cannot bear spiritual fruit apart from Christ and our relationship with Him.

I grew up on a small farm where we used to grow pumpkins, among other things. You would not believe the planning and work that goes into the growing of a pumpkin! Once the plant started to vine out, we would take a hoe and cut out the surrounding weeds to give the plant a place to grow so it would not get choked by the weeds or branches of other plants.

Sometimes while pruning the pumpkins, we would get hot and become tired because pumpkin growing season was in the middle of an Ohio summer. Of course, my siblings and I felt we had better things to do, so we would often rush to finish the task, or not pay careful attention to what we were doing. That's about the time we would hoe through one of the branches, cutting all the way through the vine or just enough to stop its growth (sorry, Dad).

As much as we tried to hide the severed branch from dad, we knew it would never be able to produce fruit. It would never get the vital nutrients it needed because it was separated from its life source. Side note: Aren't you glad that God, our Vinedresser, is never in a hurry, never gets tired of pruning us and that we will never be cut away from the vine? He is patient and loving with us and prunes us so that we can glorify Him.

We all know that a branch that is not connected to the vine will die. There is no life or any fruit of its own. All life and fruit must come from the connection of the branch to the vine. A branch is lifeless, useless, and fruitless unless it remains on the vine. It's kind of like a light not plugged into a power source. It might be a really cute lamp, but it is useless. No matter how hard you try to get that light to work, it will not work without being plugged into its power source.

The vine (God), expresses its life through the branches (us). This is an example of Christ living through us. We are to remain close to Christ in intimate connection or relationship. Christ remains in us; we remain in Him. The life of Christ (vine) becomes the life of the believer (branch). When we choose to first remain in Him, He gives us the grace and power to live the Christian life and bear HIS fruit!

So how do you remain? You do nothing but remain! It sounds so simple, but we all know it is not always easy. You remain where you find yourself, a part of the vine, placed there by God. The branch is not responsible for pruning itself. It is not responsible for other branches, which is antithetical for some of us. All a branch does is remain. When we remain, that is when we bear fruit.

We don't need to struggle to bear fruit. That's the vine's job. He is the producer of the fruit. His desires are transferred into us through daily nourishment by remaining in Him. Resting, dwelling, and remaining in Him is the only source of our strength, our goodness, our fruit. We, as the branch, have the privilege of displaying not OUR fruit, but HIS fruit.

Let's be about the business of remaining in Jesus, and trust His Spirit to be about the business of bearing fruit in our lives.

| DAY 18 |

Hidden in My Heart
Emily Sealy

In my Father's house are many mansions: if it were not so, I would have told you. I go to prepare a place for you. And if I go and prepare a place for you, I will come again, and receive you unto myself; that where I am, there ye may be also. Thomas saith unto him, Lord, we know not whither thou goest; and how can we know the way? Jesus saith unto him, I am the way, the truth, and the life: no man cometh unto the Father, but by me. - John 14:2-3, 5-6

I recently spent eight days in the hospital due to back surgery. During my stay, I was placed in a room with one other roommate. That type of situation can often lead to interesting times, but in this particular instance it turned into life lessons I will never forget. Let me explain.

She came into the room around 10 o'clock one evening. For anonymity's sake, lets call her "Vivian." She came by ambulance. She had been rushed to the hospital after her daughter witnessed her having a small stroke. They wanted to keep her for a few days to run tests and keep an eye on her, as this was her second ministroke in a week's time.

Vivian is a spunky 98-year-old woman who lived at home with her youngest daughter (who, by the way, was 71-years-old). Vivian was used to being mostly independent, but due to the strokes her left side was now paralyzed and she couldn't see out of her left eye. Yet, her spunky spirit revealed itself as she would tell jokes to the nurses and make everyone laugh.

Her mind was sharp. She remembered everyone's name. We never actually told her my name, so each morning she would call to me through the curtain dividing our beds by saying, "Good morning Next Door!" It made me smile each morning, as I yelled back, "Good morning, Vivian!" I yelled because her hearing aids weren't in so she couldn't hear me otherwise.

Vivian had a constant flow of visitors—her children and friends from her church. I could tell she was the woman in charge because she would give instructions as to what hymns she wanted sung that Sunday, as well as directing things she wanted done at home.

Everyone instantly fell in love with Vivian, myself included. You could tell she was a strong woman. But she struggled, too.

Nights were the hardest for her. When the visitors were gone, and it was quiet, she would begin to cry. What broke my heart most was that she would cry out for her Momma—a woman that had been gone for many years. She would just sob and say, "Oh Momma. This is awful. It hurts, Momma. Please come and help me!"

She would just cry and say that over and over for 30 minutes to an hour until she fell asleep. I would just lie in my bed, listening, as my heart broke. I wanted to hug her, to smooth her hair on her forehead and tell her it was going to be okay. But I couldn't walk. Instead I just laid in my bed and prayed for her.

On one particularly rough night, when her pain must have been extra intense, her cries were louder than normal. I was in the middle of praying for her when all of a sudden she stopped crying and started saying out loud:

In my Father's house are many mansions: if it were not so, I would have told you. I go to prepare a place for you. And if I go and prepare a place for you, I will come again, and receive you unto myself; that where I am, there ye may be also. Thomas saith unto him, Lord, we know not whither thou goest; and how can we know the way? Jesus saith unto him, I am the way, the truth, and the life: no man cometh unto the Father, but by me.

And then she said, "Lord, I know you are the way. I believe. I'm ready to come see you, Lord. Please take me home now! I believe." And then she quieted down and fell asleep.

I just laid there, staring into the dark room in silence. A small part of me thought that she was going to Heaven that night so I continued to pray for her.

The Lord did not take her home that night. The next couple of days were rough for her. Not long after, I was discharged and went home.

But I have not been able to get that night out of my head.

Here was this sweet old lady who had lived a long life. And even at her age, she was not free from trials and struggles. But what did she do in the midst of those struggles? She turned to God and His Word for comfort. She was in the midst of a very hard and trying time, one where she didn't know if it would ever end or what the outcome would be. And yet she knew where to find peace and strength.

Her daughter had offered to bring her Bible to her, but because of the stroke making her blind in her left eye, she couldn't really read. So she had to rely on her memory. And she quoted the *many mansions* passage perfectly, word for word.

Vivian taught me two important lessons that night.

First, she reminded me that even on the darkest night, we can call out to the Father. We can tell Him how we are feeling, how we are hurting, how we are scared. And He will bring us comfort and peace to the point that we can close our eyes and sleep.

And secondly, she taught me how important it is to have God's Word memorized. These days I think we take for granted how easily we can access our Bibles. We have multiple copies in our homes. We have apps on our phones. We can play it as an audiobook and listen to it while we are going about our day. We basically can get access to God's Word almost anywhere, anytime we want.

But that may not always be the case. One day, we may find ourselves in a situation where we won't be able to have that easy access. What then? Will we have enough in our "memory well" to draw from when we need it most?

The day I left, I told Vivian that I would be praying for her. I do not know what has become of her in the weeks since I was there. But I do know that I will always be grateful for her. She will never know the incredible testimony she was to me, or the lessons she taught me. While she was simply reaching out to God in her time of need, God was using her weakness (and His strength) to speak to my heart.

And now I want to ask you. Do you know where to go when you are in the midst of your struggle? Where you can find comfort and peace enough to go to sleep? Do you have God's Word "hidden in your heart," so that you can draw from that well at any time, anyplace?

I know that "well" is something I'm going to be working on filling, so it will be ready and full when I need it most.

| DAY 19 |

Grace
Bethany Young

For by grace are ye saved through faith; and that not of yourselves: it is the gift of God. - Ephesians 2:8

It's so freely given, so undeserved. It's what gives us freedom from our bondage, healing from our scars, hope in our darkest places, love at our messiest.

He calls us to come to Him when we are broken. He knows the true condition of our hearts, and no matter how righteous we appear, He knows our acts of righteousness are only filthy (Isaiah 64:6). And there's nothing we can ever do to reach that perfect standard. That's because He never intended us to work our way to Him (Titus 3:5, Ephesians 2:8-9).

He sent Jesus, the all righteous One. Not to condemn, but to freely give His grace (John 3:17). He came not for the righteous, but for sinners (Luke 5:32).

Come all you who are broken. He is waiting for you. Take off the mask of self righteousness, and just let His grace overwhelm you. Be free. Be healed. Be hopeful. Be loved.

Broken, but Not Forsaken
Shonda Kuehl

But Ruth said, Intreat me not to leave thee, or to return from following after thee: for whither thou goest, I will go; and where thou lodgest, I will lodge: thy people shall be my people, and thy God my God: Where thou diest, will I die, and there will I be buried: the LORD do so to me, and more also, if ought but death part thee and me. - Ruth 1:16-17

This scene in history squeezes my heart. Partly because it is just a sad part of the story of Ruth, but another part makes me feel a loss. It makes me ask, "If I were Naomi, would I have a Ruth?" 2021 is amazing because of the modern conveniences we enjoy. The electricity, the dishwasher, snow blower ... But I'm afraid in 2021 we lack commitment.

When I was a kid, I had a BFF named Chantell. We matched our clothes and wore BFF necklaces. We had sleepovers and accompanied each other on family vacations.

Even when we got on each other's nerves, we were committed. Eventually though, the commitment ran out and we went our separate ways, much like Orpah in this story.

When things get hard, we quit. When people disagree with us, we leave. When our whims are not met, we move on. Our commitment is fragile. Easily broken.

I'm glad that God is committed, and the story of Ruth is a reminder of that commitment. He has not forgotten me. I am not abandoned despite the way I sometimes feel. Have you had a time when you felt shattered? Abandoned? Forgotten?

In the midst of being shattered by false accusations and criticism, it caused me to question everything. My calling, my beliefs, my patterns, habits, convictions … desperately seeking God's Truth, His plan, and His will. God sent a message through a mentor in my time of trouble.

He did not even know what we were going through, but he sent a text to my husband and me. It was as if he knew every detail, telling us we were on the right path and to keep going. Although that man did not know the impact he would have, God knew. We saw it as God shining a ray of light on our uncertain time, giving us reassurance that He was with us in a time that seemed pretty dark.

I will not leave you comfortless: I will come to you. - John 14:18

You are not alone, God is always speaking, and offering His comfort.

Week Five

ENCOURAGEMENT FROM WOMEN

Ms. Petty and Mrs. Forbearance
Denise Peterson

Behold how good and how pleasant it is for brethren to dwell together in unity! - Psalm 133:1

I've attended many funerals. When family or friends share memories of the loved one, they always say nice things. A few times I've heard a potentially negative remark, but it is usually said in a joking manner and everyone chuckles ("Yes, Aunt Chatterbox could talk the hind legs off a mule"). Even when the person who has passed away had shortcomings, family and friends could usually find many good things to say about their departed loved one. They have decided it's not the place for little Ms. Petty to speak up. It's time for Mrs. Encouragement to speak.

During our recent mission trip to Trinidad, our team of 25 worked exceptionally well together. We stayed in quite amazing unity throughout the busy 10-day trip. Teamwork was paramount. All helped, did their part, and then did more. We were patient with each other, and encouraged one another. Because we were truly focused on the goal of reaching others with the gospel, we were able to set aside things that perhaps would normally have upset us. We were able to ignore Ms. Petty and to live and work well with Mrs. Perfect Harmony.

Ms. Petty can and wants to boss us around and fill our lives with her smallness. If our "feelings" are our primary concern, if it's "all about me," we will be hot and bothered over many things. These things, especially when viewed from a distance, are usually actually small and insignificant. Yet if we allow her, Ms. Petty can cause quite a stir and put families, coworkers or a church into complete turmoil.

While in Trinidad, we chose to focus on the big goal, and tell Ms. Petty to "Hush." We allowed Mrs. Forbearance to shine. Likewise during a funeral, when human frailty and our own mortality is staring us in the face, we again tell Ms. Petty to be quiet and consequently, Mrs. Encouragement can do her thing. After sitting through many funerals, I have made a choice to say the nice things I think about others to them while they are still breathing and it can make a big difference.

When our "feathers are ruffled," and Ms. Petty is determined to squawk (think the awful sound of sand cranes at 6:00 a.m.), we can choose to think about all the good things about the person, as if we were at their funeral. We can try to see things from the other person's perspective, to see their intent, and not just view the specific action in isolation. This may allow us to ignore Ms. Petty and allow Mrs. Patience and Mrs. Forbearance their turn to speak. If we did this, the things that others do won't steal away Mrs. Happiness, and this in turn will allow us to live comfortably with Mrs. Perfect Harmony.

Wouldn't you know it, with this article up on my desktop computer awaiting further review, something happened and it really "ruffled my feathers!" I was hot and bothered. I found myself stewing away in my little pity party juices. "How could they?" But, I caught myself and realized I was allowing Little Ms. Petty to squawk and when I realized it, I actually laughed at how silly it was to be writing this article and feel like I felt. So…I took my own medicine, and even though it tasted a bit bitter on the way down, I was soon able to be back in fellowship with Mrs. Forbearance and Mrs. Encouragement.

It's practically impossible to be friends with Ms. Petty and Mrs. Forbearance and Mrs. Encouragement all at the same time. We need to let Ms. Petty go. Unfriend her on the Facebook of your mind. She's really not worth the aggravation.

Behold, how good and how pleasant it is for brethren to dwell together in unity! - Psalm 133:1

Worship. Fight. Repeat.
McKenzie Jones

The voice of one crying in the wilderness, Prepare ye the way of the Lord, make his paths straight. John did baptize in the wilderness, and preach the baptism of repentance for the remission of sins.

And preached, saying, There cometh one mightier than I after me, the latchet of whose shoes I am not worthy to stoop down and unloose.

And it came to pass in those days, that Jesus came from Nazareth of Galilee, and was baptized of John in Jordan. And straightway coming up out of the water, he saw the heavens opened, and the Spirit like a dove descending upon him: And there came a voice from heaven, saying, Thou art my beloved Son, in whom I am well pleased. - Mark 1:3-4, 7, 9-11

John was an amazing follower of Jesus, and although he felt unworthy to baptize Jesus, he had to be super excited about getting to do so. Talk about a ministry highlight! But then, fast forward just a bit, and we soon see John in the depth's of despair (in prison) questioning if Jesus was the Messiah. *When the men were come unto him (Jesus), they said, John Baptist hath sent us unto thee, saying, Art thou he that should come? or look we for another?*- Luke 7:20

Yikes, what kind of follower of Jesus was he? If he were alive today, no doubt Christians would have questioned his salvation and many blog posts would have been written about his ministry failures. He seems to have such measly faith for a guy who, all at once, saw the heavens opened, the Spirit of God descend like a dove, and heard the voice of God while baptizing God in human flesh. But you see, now, John's in prison for telling Herod some hard truths; and unbeknownst to him, he's about to be beheaded. Many times living for Jesus looks a lot more like dying (at least to self). And if I'm honest, I'm not a fan, but I'm learning to be.

I like to see the victories! Yes to all the miracles! Cue the praise hands.

But, if we we're completely honest, we look a lot like John the Baptist. When our victories turn into more battles, we're over here like … do we look for another … another plan, a better situation? We forget Who is in control. If we don't stay on guard during an enemy attack, even Christians can start saying, "God I'm not sure you're good … or dare I say it … even real." Wow! That can spiral out of control so quickly.

Have you been there? Are you in a prison of doubt and despair now. You don't have to stay. Unless, you're actually in a real prison. But, you can rejoice even there as God encourages your heart and strengthens you by His Spirit.

I have found these things to be incredibly helpful right after a major spiritual victory. Worshiping, fighting, and repeating the process helps keep me on track.

•Worship

You didn't minister successfully because of your goodness or win a spiritual battle because of your strength. It's time to worship and give the glory to the {ONE} to Whom it belongs. Be thankful, and stay humble. *But he giveth more grace. Wherefore he saith, God resisteth the proud, but giveth grace unto the humble. Submit yourselves therefore to God. Resist the devil, and he will flee from you.* - James 4:6-7

•Fight

Get ready to fight. You need to put on your armor (Ephesians 6) because Satan is waiting for an opportunity to trip you up right after a victory AND … be aware. You can be your own worst enemy in the spiritual fight. If you are not giving in to what might be considered "bad sin," you could be in dangerous territory for giving in to the also bad sin of stupid {PRIDE}.

I may be reading into this way too much, but I find it interesting. The next time we find John the Baptist, after he baptized Jesus, he was making bold declarations to Herod. (P.S. They were true, but I just kind of wonder if he would have been more effective calling Herod's attentions to repentance and Jesus.) *For John had said unto Herod, It is not lawful for thee to have thy brother's wife.* - Mark 6:18

We are not the morality police for the lost world. We are the preachers of the Gospel. The Gospel fixes everything-literally. AND … The Holy Spirit is the morality police for the believer. The Bible tells us to encourage one another, as believers, to love and good works. So, we can definitely share godly advice, but Galatians 6:1 gives us a really great template for what that looks like.

• **Repeat**

Then Jesus answering said unto them, Go your way, and tell John what things ye have seen and heard; how that the blind see, the lame walk, the lepers are cleansed, the deaf hear, the dead are raised, to the poor the gospel is preached. And blessed is he, whosoever shall not be offended in me.

But what went ye out for to see? A prophet? Yea, I say unto you, and much more than a prophet.

For I say unto you, Among those that are born of women there is not a greater prophet than John the Baptist: but he that is least in the kingdom of God is greater than he. - Luke 7:22-23, 26, 28

Think about Jesus' encouragement to and about doubting John. Jesus was still doing miracles, and John was the greatest prophet. Yep ... so strange yet so encouraging! Have you been in a battle? Worship.

Have you been in a prison of defeat? Be honest with God about what you're feeling, and put your armor on and fight.

Daily tip: When a victory comes, give glory to God; and be on guard for enemy attacks. Then, ask yourself if you're okay if victory is defined by God rather than you!

When Your Deepest Pain Becomes Your Greatest Ministry Connection
Kimberly Coombes

Remember ye not the former things, neither consider the things of old. Behold, I will do a new thing: now it shall spring forth; shall ye not know it? I will even make a way in the wilderness, and rivers in the desert. - Isaiah 43:18-19

I was sexually assaulted.

Just saying those words makes me catch my breath and want to hide.

Saying that in a public forum like this devotional.............terrifying.

But like it or not, it is a piece of my story and refusing to acknowledge it certainly didn't make it go away.

For years that's exactly what it was. Mine, my story, my secret — that I held close with a suffocating grip.

Then, I shared it with my soon to be husband, positive it would come up one day in our married life. I was convinced he was going to leave me and should have the freedom to do so before we were married – He didn't.

Then, God began to move me along in my healing journey and impressed upon my heart to share it with my pastor. One problem, he's not just my pastor, he's my husband's boss. I was convinced he would fire my husband – He didn't.

I kept walking. Kept healing. Kept hoping. Once again God began to nudge my heart, this time to tell my small group. I was convinced they would despise me and pull away from friendships – They didn't.

But what did happen was women, oh so many women, began coming to me desperate to share their stories with someone who would understand; someone they could trust. I began getting phone calls, text messages, and personal invitations to counsel with women who, like me, had carried a painful secret for far too long and were looking for someone who could sit with them in their pain and show them how Jesus is Greater, how He is Better, and how He is a beautiful Healer. And God began to show me that where I hurt the deepest and wanted to hide the most was exactly the place where He wanted me to meet with other women and point them to Him.

What pain can you lay on the altar of sacrifice today?
- Coming from a broken home
- A failed marriage
- A miscarriage
- An abortion
- An assault

Who needs you to sit with them, not in your perfection, but in your point of suffering to help lead them to a beautiful Savior?

Isaiah 43:18-19 *Remember ye not the former things, neither consider the things of old. Behold, I will do a new thing: now it shall spring forth; shall ye not know it? I will even make a way in the wilderness, and rivers in the desert.*

| DAY 24 |

Discovering My Identity
Irene Castaneda

Trust in the LORD with all thine heart; and lean not unto thine own understanding. In all thy ways acknowledge him, and he shall direct thy paths. - Proverbs 3:5-6

Unloved. Disliked. Weird. Awkward. Ugly. Too attached. Socially awkward. Fake.

These are lies that run through my head constantly. One minute I'll be fine and the next, something happens that triggers one of these lies to run through my head. I start to overthink situations and assume the worst. I'll hear from one of my friends what other people think about me and it will automatically become a label I paste on myself. This is something I struggled with almost daily up until recently when I discovered my true identity. I worried too much about what other people thought of me and I allowed these cowards to control my emotions.

Philippians 4:8 would come into my mind but I had a hard time thinking about what's true and lovely because my mind was so clouded. It's not something I wanted to let control me but I always felt like I had no way out. I'd cry at night just listening to all the lies I assumed people thought about me. I would read my Bible or a short devotional on my phone before I went to bed just because I knew it was the right thing to do, but I didn't always learn something. I didn't want to talk to anyone about how I felt because I thought they'd tell me I was just feeling selfish and wanted attention but that was SO wrong. I ended up being asked to be a counselor for my church's teen camp and I was excited to go because I knew that every year at camp the preaching always spoke to me and seemed to help me reconnect with God.

The first full day of camp was evidence that God works everything for good to those who love Him and are called by Him. The preacher spoke on depression and how to escape it when all seems lost. It was at that moment that I realized that, if for no other reason, I was at camp to hear that message. The pastor gave some reasons why people get depressed — finances, lies, friends, health, or even genetics. He talked about how David was a man after God's own heart yet he was one of the most depressed people in the Bible.

Over and over again in Psalms we see the psalmists crying out to God asking for deliverance and comfort. In Psalm 42, the psalmist says, *"As the hart (deer) panteth after the water brooks, so panteth my soul after thee, O God."* He goes on to ask when God will take him home so he can see Him and how his tears make him question where He is. Later the psalmist continues, *Yet the LORD will command his loving kindness in the daytime, and in the night his song shall be with me, and my prayer unto the God of my life.*

The psalmist recognizes that God is with him every step of the way even if it doesn't always seem like it. Jesus knows our troubles and our difficulties. The way to get out of our depressed state is to find hope in God and praise Him. Hope is not wishing, it's KNOWING that things are going to get better and KNOWING that God will deliver us and that He has a better future planned for us then we could ever imagine. Don't focus on the now.

Philippians 4:6-9 reads, *Be careful for nothing; but in everything by prayer and supplication with thanksgiving let your requests be made known unto God. And the peace of God, which passeth all understanding, shall keep your hearts and minds through Christ Jesus. Finally, brethren, whatsoever things are true, whatsoever things are honest, whatsoever things are pure, whatsoever things are lovely, whatsoever things are of good report; if there be any virtue, and if there be any praise, think on these things. Those things which ye have both learned, and received, and heard, and seen in me, do: and the God of peace shall be with you.*

So how can we be delivered from depression?

1) Know that God will deliver you and He has something amazing planned for your life.

2) Sing praises when you don't feel like it until you do feel like it.

3) Look in the mirror every day and find one good thing about yourself and remind yourself of that truth throughout the day.

You are loved, you are strong, you are beautiful, you are caring, you are kind, you are forgiven, you are valued, you are a daughter of the One true King which makes you royalty...YOU'RE A PRINCESS for crying out loud! Soak in these truths and whenever Satan tries to creep into your head and make you feel worthless stop the lie right there, ask God to fill your head with truth, and repeat that truth in your head until the lies go away.

Sometimes Satan uses lies to attack some of God's strongest soldiers because he thinks that if he can keep them from doing their best for God that he's won.

Lastly, talk to someone about the depression you're struggling with. Find someone you know who will listen to you without criticizing, pray for you, and remind you of your worth. I finally talked with one of my friends about how I felt so alone and unloved and she helped me through it by reminding me of how loved I am by not only God, but everyone around me. She filled my head with the truth about how she felt toward me and assured me that many others felt the same way. You see, often the lies we hear about ourselves are just that, LIES.

Learn to ignore the lies and discover your identity in Christ. Read a psalm to remind yourself that you aren't the only one who feels alone, and that God WILL deliver you.

Psalm 61:2, tells us what to do when we are overwhelmed by our emotions, including depression. *From the end of the earth will I cry unto thee, when my heart is overwhelmed: lead me to the rock that is higher than I.*

Crank up the music that reminds you of God's love and how He values you and let those words sink deep into your mind. Don't give up on yourself because God has not and will not give up on you. Direct your mind with hope and your mouth with praise.

Trafficking: When God Speaks
Christi Wells

Humble yourselves therefore under the mighty hand of God, that he may exalt you in due time. - 1 Peter 5:6

When I was a chid, I wanted to be a famous singer. Growing up in the 1980's, I had my cassette tapes of all sorts of Christian artists. Pursuing a music degree was part of my plan to follow that dream. One day in college, while reading 1 Peter 5:6, God clearly spoke to my heart, "Don't seek to exalt yourself, let ME be in control of that. You follow me." So, I changed my major and surrendered my dreams of being on stage for a career in the classroom, which I dearly loved!

For a time, life was simple. I married the man of my dreams and gave up teaching to start a family. A few years later, God spoke to me again. Following His voice, I started a program called *Raise the Standard*. It included writing curricula and guest speaking in schools, all while being a stay-at-home mom. God opened doors for us to partner with a Christian ministry that helps women escape sex trafficking. I began writing more curricula and speaking on topics of sexual abuse, sex trafficking, pornography, and healthy relationships. Children are being trafficked in virtually every small town in America. The average age for entering sex trafficking in the US is 12-14 years old. Soon, I found myself speaking in schools, churches, on college campuses, and at conferences on stages in front of large audiences. God was bringing me back to my dream of being on stage, but not how I had imagined.

HIS plan was NOT what I expected, but through it, I have learned some important lessons. First of all, the passion that He gave me to be in front of people was not wrong. It was a gift! God was stirring my heart in order to prepare me for the ministry I'm in now. God knew and simply asked me to trust Him.

Sweet friend, you have a gift! I don't know what it is, but likely, it's what you are most passionate about. It may be crocheting, blogging, working in the corporate scene, or being a stay-at-home mom. Can I say a word to you? Enjoy the journey. Do what you love to do and do it for God's glory to the best of your ability. Acknowledge your talents, use them to follow hard after God, and let Him direct you in His time. I promise, His plan is better than yours. Sometimes there's a wait and sometimes even suffering, but God is strengthening you for His purpose and will settle you.

1 Peter 5:10 *But the God of all grace, who hath called us unto his eternal glory by Christ Jesus, after that ye have suffered a while, make you perfect, stablish, strengthen, settle you.*

Week Six

ENCOURAGEMENT FROM WOMEN

| DAY 26 |

Pouring Happiness
Dawn Suttle

Seeing then that all these things shall be dissolved, what manner of persons ought ye to be in all holy conversation and godliness. - 2 Peter 3:11

"When you decide to 'show up' consistently as the best version of who you are, it gives you the opportunity to meet people where they are and you never know when people need you to be your very best." Ryan Estis, Certified Human Capital Strategist

The story below caught my attention and has stayed with me since the first time I heard it. I have determined to 'Show up/React' with my best self. I challenge you to do the same.

Ryan stepped up to the counter to order coffee shortly after he arrived at the airport. He was greeted with a very warm and sincere welcome.

"Hi my name is Lily, what's yours?" the barista asked. "Ryan", he replied. "Ryan, what can I make for you today?" Lily asked. "I'll have a Grande pumpkin spice latte." Lily smiled and said, "Tell you what, I'm gonna make it extra hot and load it up with whip cream and spread a little nutmeg on top! You are gonna LOVE it." "Sounds great", Ryan said. "Where are you going?" "Cleveland" Ryan replied. "Are you going to see family for the holidays?" Lily then began asking questions about Ryan's family and their holiday traditions. The two bantered back and forth laughing. Then Lily handed Ryan his coffee and said, "Ryan, have a safe trip back to Cleveland, go create some extraordinary memories and on your return trip, stop by to let me know all about it."

Surprised that she had created within him a desire to return and tell Lily of his visit, Ryan had to ask her, "What is your secret to making such meaningful connections over serving coffee?" She corrected Ryan, "Ryan, I am not serving coffee … I am pouring happiness into people's lives."

Here is what the barista had learned: She wanted to be happy, to be around happy people, to care about her customers, to want them to come back, so she CHOSE to smile, to have fun, to help people, and to JUST BE HAPPY.

Ladies, we all have good days and not-so-good days. The trick to success is not a trick at all but a solid determination to let the Holy Spirit control our emotions and actions. Quite often a deep breath—or maybe even a mini Snickers bar—gives us that fraction of a second we need to gather ourselves in order to pray, think, and respond appropriately.

We DO make that CHOICE every day and in a million ways. Let's stand on Scripture, 2 Peter 3:11 and Philippians 4:4, as the source of our resolve to be the best that we can be—at all times.

| DAY 27 |

A Truly Successful Woman
Sierra Fedorko

But they measuring themselves by themselves, and comparing themselves among themselves, are not wise. – 2 Corinthians 10:12

Have you ever asked yourself these questions:

- What is success?

- How do I live my life well?

- How do I not get overwhelmed by all the self-help books, Instagram lingo, and Christian catchphrases?

It's so easy to exhaust ourselves with these questions, adopt the new and shiniest lifestyle habits, compare our lives to others, or just compare our lives to how we think our lives should be right now. Good things like success and self-improvement can actually become destructive to our living freely, fully, and well. Why? Because it's so easy for us to become obsessed with ourselves and with our progress (or the lack of it).

What's the solution? How do we not get overwhelmed by all the noise on social media and in our lives?

1. Reframe your picture of success!

A truly successful woman is a wise woman who trusts God, obeys God, and knows that God will finish His work in her, and will fulfill His purpose for her. Resting in what God will do in your life doesn't give you an excuse to sit around and twiddle your thumbs, but it does mean you will be full of peace as you go about obeying + trusting God with your life! (Proverbs 3:5-6, Psalm 138:8)

2. Remember God has specific work for you to do! (Ephesians 2:10)

When we serve God with our lives, it is not us reaching for His love and grace, it is us responding to His love and grace already in our lives. So how do we do the work we are called to do today?

Be in God's Word, renew your mind by dwelling on what is true, and pray to God for help and wisdom. In doing this, your eyes will be opened to people who need encouragement, tasks you could be doing more thoroughly, things in life you need to surrender to God, and your time that could be better used elsewhere. When you're in fellowship with God, you will know what it means to obey Him with your life and you will recognize the ministry that's already in front of you! Suddenly, it won't matter what she's doing or what you could be doing if only you had this, that, or the other. Why? Because you are content to serve God with all of you and all you have—even if it doesn't look exciting or shiny.

3. Focus on cultivating your relationship with God.

When you pursue the heart of God, you will (in His strength) obey Him, you will walk through big problems with a peace of mind, tackle tough situations without giving up, and live unswayed by society's pressure. Instead of trying to be the best, you will simply offer your best work, goals, and dreams to God . . . however they look right now.

True success is obeying God with your life, trusting God with your life, and resting in God for the outcome of your life. Keep this in mind and all the noise in your life will either die out or take its proper place! Go live confidently, because in God you can!

What Does Your Dash Look Like Today?
Cindy Wicks

Whereas ye know not what shall be on the morrow. For what is your life? It is even a vapour, that appeareth for a little time, and then vanisheth away. - James 4:14

One day, my tombstone will read...

Cindy Wicks
April 9, 1985 - 20??
A loving wife, mother, and friend.

(At least I hope that's what my epitaph will say.)

I don't really remember my birth, but I know God planned the day I was to be born.

I definitely don't know the day of my death. That, too, is in God's hands.

The thing I do know is that I have control over that dash between the dates. We've heard famous poets muse about that dash in our lives. The question is, what does your dash look like right now?

Death has a funny way of helping us put things into perspective.

If today were the last day of my dash, I wouldn't get so upset at my kiddos over silly things. I would have taken more time to talk with my neighbor. I would have said "I love you" more. I would have maybe put a little more love into that lunch I made for my husband. I would have spent a lot more time with the Lord. I wouldn't live in fear over life's simple problems. I would be more thankful. I would be more patient. I would be more understanding. I wouldn't be so anxious. I would take the day and embrace it. *Carpe diem*, "seize the day." Don't put off until tomorrow the love you can show others today!

What is it in your life today that you know you should let go of and give to God so that you can live out your dash in a way that is Christ honoring and glorifying to Him?

Daily Tip: Let's make the most of our dash today.

Ex-Gay Awareness Month
By Sarah Adler

Therefore if any man be in Christ, he is a new creature: old things are passed away; behold, all things are become new.
– 2 Corinthians 5:17

A friend of mine recently shared that September is "Ex-Gay Awareness Month." If you had met me in 2009-2014 you probably would have met my then-current girlfriend as well. You might have made a comment about homosexuality being sinful, and I would have verbally attacked you with a profanity laced response. You might have shared the Gospel with me, and I would have belittled your "mythical sky daddy" and "fictitious *book* used to brainwash people and control their lives." I loved my lifestyle and I hated anyone who told me it or I was wrong!

One evening in November of 2014 I was dining out with a friend. The "Nosy Nancy" sitting behind me obviously heard part of our conversation and turned around and struck up a brief conversation. After a few moments she invited me to visit her church. We exchanged phone numbers and I committed to give it a shot. Later, I wondered why I had told her I would attend. Doesn't sound like me, I thought. But I took pride in my commitment as I reassured myself that one doesn't have to be a goody-two-shoes heterosexual *Christian* to keep one's word!

As Sunday drew closer, I was increasingly anxious because I knew what "people like that" thought about "people like me." When I first started attending church I told everyone quite unabashedly that I was a lesbian. I sort of dared them to tell me I was wrong. They didn't. I was waiting for the pastor to preach against homosexuality or to call me out otherwise. He didn't. I was waiting for someone to tell me I was going to burn in hell for all eternity. No one did.

A few weeks after my first attendance, I emailed the pastor and asked to meet with someone who could explain how I, a practicing lesbian, could be saved. I met with the Assistant Pastor and his wife who shared the Gospel and led me to the Lord. As God began sanctifying me, I learned that my identity is found in Christ - not in my sexual preference. I learned that when I prayed, God heard me. I learned that God desires to conform us to the image of His Son, and that growing in the Gospel is a lifelong journey.

It was comforting to hear other believers freely admit their sinfulness rather than focus on mine. When I accepted Christ, I expected that my attraction to women would vanish immediately and was disappointed when it did not. A friend of mine suggested that I ask God to remove the sinful desires of my heart and replace them with desires that were pleasing to Him. I followed her advice. Shortly thereafter I received a message from a woman I had previously been "madly in love" with. She wanted to see me. I politely told her I wasn't interested. It was at that point that I realized God had given me a new heart as He had promised to do. A heart which desires things that are pleasing to Him, a heart that strives to honor Him, a heart to follow Him.

God really is a miracle worker. When we are faithful and pray according to His will, He hears and answers us. I am forever thankful that He saved me from my sin through the shed blood of His Son and that I can rest knowing that I will spend eternity in heaven with Him.

If you know others who are struggling with same-sex attraction, I implore you to treat them the same as you would any other lost soul in need of salvation. Focus on their hearts, not their "sin of choice." Treat them like a person, not a project. Paul tells us in Romans 2:4 that it is the goodness of God that leads a person to repentance. Thank God that the Assistant Pastor and his wife who led me to the Lord understood this. Our job as Christians is to share the Gospel and provide lost souls with the opportunity to put their faith in Jesus Christ. God will take care of the rest.

Philippians 1:6 assures us, *Being confident of this very thing, that he which hath begun a good work in you will perform it until the day of Jesus Christ.*

Whose You Are
Kathy Whittenburg

But as many as received him, to them gave he power to become the sons (and daughters) of God, even to them that believe on his name. - John 1:12

About four years ago, I was asked to do a skit for a ladies' conference at our church. The skit was a ten-minute monologue about a day in the life of a mom. To begin the skit, I stood on the platform wearing a sleeping cap. A fake baby in a carrier was strapped to my chest. The "day" started and immediately I switched into a drill sergeants cap where I rallied the troops for rise and shine — demanding their name, rank, and cereal preferences.

After the kids and husband were sent off to school my hat switched again to a "cow" hat as I attempted to feed the fake baby attached to me. Quickly, the hats changed again, and a fireman's hat replaced the cow hat. My toddler had climbed onto the fridge and needed to be rescued! The nursing hat came on quickly after that, as I had to kiss a boo-boo, and make all things right again in the world for my adventurous boy.

Soon after, I switched into a cleaning hat and began tackling the days household chores. Before I knew it, my chauffeur's hat was on and I was running around, gathering the children from school. While driving and singing "Let it Go" at the top of my lungs, the phone rings. It's my husband. He's calling to let me know that he's bringing the Pastor and his wife over for dinner. They'll be here in 30 minutes!

I run my invisible car through the drive-through at KFC and hurry home to put on my chef's hat. Quickly, and not with the best attitude, as my fake children are fighting and destroying my fake home, I place all of the items for our dinner on the table, switch into my Sunday bonnet and slap a giant fake smile onto my face. I enjoy conversation and compliments over my fabulous home cooked meal, and then send our guests home for the evening.

My husband gets the kids ready for bed as my cleaning hat comes back on, then the cow hat and then finally the sleeping cap. I start to fall into a blissful sleep when I am awakened by someone calling me. I jump up from my sleep saying "What? Who? Who needs me now?!?" That's when I look over at my invisible husband and well … I ended the skit in a pink, feather boa saying "ooo la la" while I shimmied across the platform—obviously, one of my best moments.

Do your days look like this? We run around fulfilling the roles our "hats" demand.
We are Wives
Mothers
Chauffeurs
Sisters
Daughters
Friends
Neighbors

We are teachers
Coaches
Nurses
Bosses
Employees
Caregivers
We are So. Many. Things. Oftentimes we find ourselves changing our hats so fast that we forget who WE are. Our identities get lost in the titles that we hold. If we aren't careful, we will start focusing on WHAT we are, or what we think we should be.

We are NOT
An Instagram filter
A Facebook like
A retweet
A Tick Tock video
Just a Pinterest worthy party-thrower

We are NOT
Just an abuse victim
A forgotten friendship
A barren wife
Just an abandoned child
A number on a scale
A diagnosis
A rank in a company
Just an unmarried or divorced woman

It isn't about WHO we are, it isn't about WHAT we are or are not.
We need to remember WHOSE we are.

You are a child of GOD.

John 1:12 assures us, *But as many as received him, to them gave he power to become the sons (and daughters) of God, even to them that believe on his name.*
Galatians 3:26 reminds us that we are children of God by faith in Jesus Christ.

You are a daughter of the KING
Psalm 45: 9-14

You are a joint-heir with CHRIST
Romans 8:17

With these titles come a whole host of new "hats"-
Forgiven – Colossians 3:13
Redeemed – Psalm 31:5
Loved – 1 John 4:19 / Jeremiah 31:3
Chased – Psalm 23:6
Lead – Psalm 119:105
Protected – Psalm 46:1
Helped – Isaiah 41:13
Known – Psalm 139:1
Remembered – Psalm 103:14
Chosen – 1 Peter 2:9

Our lives move fast, our schedules get packed, our hats are many. In the midst of being WHO God made us to be, doing WHAT He made us to do, let's not forget WHOSE we are, as we live to glorify Him every day.

Application: Today when you are "doing" everything you have to, remember Whose you are while you're doing it! You are more than just … you are a child of the King!

Bonus Days

Grow Out of It
Blandy Mendoza

Till we all come in the unity of the faith, and of the knowledge of the Son of God, unto a perfect man, unto the measure of the stature of the fulness of Christ: That we henceforth be no more children, tossed to and fro, and carried about with every wind of doctrine, by the sleight of men, and cunning craftiness, whereby they lie in wait to deceive; But speaking the truth in love, may grow up into him in all things, which is the head, even Christ: From whom the whole body fitly joined together and compacted by that which every joint supplieth, according to the effectual working in the measure of every part, maketh increase of the body unto the edifying of itself in love. -
Ephesians 4:13-16

I remember that trip home from the beach like it was yesterday. We had enjoyed a fun-filled day as a family and we were eager to get home and rest. During the drive, I noticed my 18 month-old scratching the back of his knees and wiggling uncomfortably in his car seat. When we arrived home, I checked him and sure enough there were huge patches of red, blotchy irritation on the back of his legs. The next day we visited the doctor and he let us know that our little one had a common skin condition called eczema. He assured us that with proper care it was manageable, and that he should grow out of it in time.

Well, that little 18 month-old is now ten years old and

I can attest to the fact that after all the doctor visits, prescription creams, oatmeal baths, and special diet restrictions, he hasn't had an outbreak in years. The other day as I cleaned out a drawer that used to house his many remedies, I remembered those words our doctor had told us years ago: "He should grow out of it." In that moment, I was so thankful that our little one had indeed grown out of it, but then I was challenged by the same thought.

Many common childhood ailments are expected to be a "stage" or a temporary condition that they will eventually grow out of, and for the most part they do. In the same way, God's Word admonishes us to grow out of "childish things," to grow in grace, faith, love, and unity with one another.

There are many Christian women today who are still dealing with the same spiritual immaturity that they should have outgrown years ago. Many of us still struggle with disciplining our lives in ways that will bring greater honor and glory to God. Perhaps we still display jealousy, bursts of anger, laziness in our daily time in the Word, unforgiveness, or evil speaking. Perhaps we have never restored a relationship that we know should have been restored, because of our pride. Maybe we continue to have the same negative attitude toward our circumstances, or we refuse to step out in obedience to a calling God has placed on our hearts because of fear.

Sweet sister, as James says, this aught not be so. The maturing of our faith is of paramount importance to the cause of Christ here on earth. Through our spiritual growth as women, wives, mothers, sisters, daughters, and friends, we help build up the Kingdom of God. When we grow out of spiritual immaturity we help build unity in our relationships at home. Those unified relationships at home inspire unified relationships with those in our community, our circle of influence, and our churches. Growing women build strong, unified families, and strong, unified families build strong, unified churches. Strong, unified churches build up the Kingdom of God!

What a glorious thought it is to know that if we do our part to grow out of our spiritual immaturities, we will increase the unity in the body of Christ. That unity is then a beautiful testimony to a lost and dying world that needs Jesus more than anything else in this life. Growing Christians grow Christians.

So, as we examine our lives today, are we still dealing with the same heart issues that we did years ago? Are we still fighting the same fights, arguing the same arguments, lacking the same self-control? Or have we, by the grace of God, grown out of those behaviors and thereby increased our effectiveness and productivity for the cause of Christ? Whatever your spiritual challenge is, are you growing out of it?

Daily Tip: Take time to meditate on any areas of your life that may need some spiritual maturing. Write them down in a journal along with Ephesians 4:13-16. Whenever you find yourself displaying an immature behavior tell yourself to "Grow out of it." Remember that growing in this area will not only make you a more joyful Christian, but it will help build God's Kingdom!

Biological Clocks and Burning Questions
Courtney Holloway Montgomery

To every thing there is a season, and a time to every purpose under the heavens. - Ecclesiastes 3:1

One Christmas, my dad thought it would be a great idea if my sister and I went through all our childhood storage bins cluttering his shed. When you have five children, things tend to pile up and when they live all over the country (Arizona, Hawaii, Florida, etc.) they don't always have the space — or desire— to take all their childhood mementos with them. In any case, my sister and I started sorting through piles of printed pics (who does that anymore?), old Clinique gift bags, books, handwritten letters from high school friends, and Hello Kitty diaries full of anguish.

We had a good laugh reading second grade missives about getting on each others nerves and playground battles with fifth grade bullies. It was funny to read long letters about unrequited love and being misunderstood by guys that we were just "talking to" at the time. Oh, the '90's were a great time to be a kid!

Now that my sister and I are happily married to great guys, it is easy to look back and laugh about relationships that didn't work out. Hindsight is 20/20 as they say and we now have the benefit of knowing more of the story. If there is one thing I could tell my younger self, it would be not to waste time worrying about whether I would get a date to an Artist Series in college or whether that guy in the church singles group has potential. Thankfully, our parents never pushed us to get married right after college.

For Christian girls, marriage is often portrayed as the highest goal. Those who don't get married are relegated to the singles group and are often peppered with questions by well-meaning people at church about why/how they are still single. For most, marriage may be part of God's plan for their lives. However, that is not always the case (see the life of the Apostle Paul). Judging by my own journal entries, I often worried about never meeting anyone or whether certain life decisions (moving to Hawaii after college or later to Washington, DC) would help or hurt my chances in the boyfriend department.

Looking back, I can see how God ordered my steps throughout every stage of my life. Despite the high school angst and the fact that I was almost 30 when I got married, it all worked out and I had some really great opportunities to meet people and travel along the way.

My husband and I actually went to college together and graduated in the same class (2005). We had mutual acquaintances but never dated back then. Even though he was from Illinois and I was from South Carolina and he moved to Kansas City and I moved to Hawaii after graduation, we ended up getting married in 2014. #providence

Though I wouldn't have planned it that way, thankfully, God knew best. We wouldn't trade our experiences apart. We did date long distance forever (it seemed that way at the time) but even that (though it was hard) was part of the plan.

Of course, now all the questions are about when we are going to start a family. If we did have a child then all the questions would be about whether we would give him/her a sibling and so it goes. People are nothing if not predictable.

I have always taken comfort in the fact that whatever God has for me is for me. Wasting time worrying about whether or not things are happening on my timetable is just that—a waste of time. God's plans are best even when we can't see how it will all work out.

"Single life may be only a stage of a life's journey, but even a stage is a gift. God may replace it with another gift, but the receiver accepts His gifts with thanksgiving. This gift for this day. The life of faith is lived one day at a time, and it has to be lived—not always looked forward to as though the 'real' living were around the next corner. It is today for which we are responsible. God still owns tomorrow." - Elisabeth Elliot, Christian author and speaker (1926—2015)

| DAY 33 |

The Stony Path
Tamah Bryant

Being confident of this very thing, that he which hath begun a good work in you will perform it until the day of Jesus Christ. - Phillippians 1:6

Not sure when or where I lost myself, but somewhere along life's way I became somebody else, somebody I hardly even recognize, somebody I hardly even know.

Guilty...
Frustrated...
Constantly worried about what other people think. I see someone who looks angry, sad, disappointed. I think, "What did I do? It must be my fault." Frustrated because I want to make it right, but I don't know how. Worried that it will only get worse. My chest tightens, tears sting my eyes. I cannot let anybody see me like this. I hide until I have control of myself. Why am I so weak? Why can't I hold myself together? Why are my emotions always all over the place? Get control of yourself. Take a deep breath, dry your eyes, and leave your room. You are going to be all right. Put a smile on your face and get back to work. People are talking to me. What are they saying? Why can't I understand? Why can't I make myself understand what they are saying? Where are my words? Why am I so awkward? I get nervous and I say the dumbest things, my tongue gets tied and my mind doesn't work as fast as my mouth does. Find a way out and

disappear until you get it together! Where did my personality go? Where am I? What happened to me? I find a quiet place, I need to be alone. I need to hear myself think. I need to remember who I am.

I close my eyes, I see a path, I am scared, I am alone, I am vulnerable. I see myself take my first step. It is dark — so very dark. I stumble over a rock. As I pick myself up, I notice that I am bleeding. I hold my arm, the crimson life spilling from my wound. I look again at the path, it is so dark. Something draws my gaze up and I see a Light, far off in the distance. The warm glow of the Light is the most beautiful thing I have ever seen. I am so cold. I am so sad. The Light brightens the path I am on just a little, it looks so hard, there are so many obstacles. There are so many enemies. I hear them talking...

"You are not good enough..."
"You are not smart enough..."
"You are not righteous enough..."
"You are not holy enough..."
"You do not trust God enough..."
"You are not there for your family enough..."
"You do not do enough..."

"ENOUGH!" I scream, holding my ears as I fall to the ground. "Enough." I sob as I will myself to quit. I am so tired, I am hurting, I am lonely. I just need to rest. I hear a voice, is it coming from the Light? "Come unto me, I will give you rest." Could that be true? Why would anything so beautiful ever want me? "I don't know if I can, I am so tired," I respond. The Light answers back, "I give power to the faint, I will increase your strength." I get back up and I am resolved. The Light becomes brighter, I start to walk around the stones but I am still being attacked. The words I hear pierce me like arrows, it feels as though my heart is breaking as I hear again, "You are not enough!" As I pray to the Light for strength, I open my eyes and notice there is a breastplate across my chest. RIGHTEOUSNESS.

"My child, you do not have to be enough because I have clothed you in My righteousness and I Am enough, I Am more than enough."

Slowly, peace starts to replace the agonizing feeling in my heart. But I still hear that voice, not as strong but still unsettling. "You cannot do this." I stop. I will myself to stand still. I raise my face toward the Light. Feelings of resolve and commitment wash over me as the Light warms my face. "You can do all things through CHRIST who gives you strength!"

As I stand there listening to the voice in the Light, I feel a belt wrap around my waist. TRUTH.

I look down at my feet as combat boots ready for battle appear on my tired and bleeding feet. GOSPEL OF PEACE.

I have shoes that are ready for battle and yet, here I stand. I do feel stronger now, but will it last? Can I really do this? My mind is filled with doubt.

"I began this good work in you and I will complete it."

I look down at my hands and see that I am holding a shield. FAITH.

"It is You who is working through me, it is You who will fight for me, I need only to be still!" A wave of confidence surges through my soul.

I feel a helmet being placed on my head, SALVATION. My thoughts are more clear than they have ever been. My mind is safe. I can no longer hear the voices shouting at me, taunting me.

I touch my helmet and make sure it is secure. I run my hand across my shield of faith. A tear runs down my cheek and lands on the most beautiful shoes I have ever worn and I thank the Light for the Gospel that brings me such peace even though there is war all around me. I place my hand firmly upon my Breastplate of Righteousness and tug on my Belt of Truth. My armor is in place and I lift my hands in praise and worship of my God, my Light. As I lower my hands I see they are no longer empty, but are now holding a sword. SPIRIT.

"Now pray, pray like you have never prayed before! Righteous and fervent prayers avail much. So be still and know that I am God—and pray!"

As I start to pray, I see a legion of angels soar through the air above me. The enemy pelts me with fiery darts, but they can't penetrate my armor. Demons start dropping at my feet, their words silenced. I start to walk down the stony path toward the Light.

One by one the stones disappear. The path is clear, it is narrow and steep, but it is clear. "Now walk." As I start on my journey, the Light that had been in the distance is now surrounding me. "You are not alone, I am with you, I will never leave you. You will never be alone." I whisper softly through grateful and humble tears. "Your grace is sufficient for me."

I Am NOT Enough
Jen McGee

Of such an one will I glory: yet of myself I will not glory, but in mine infirmities. For though I would desire to glory, I shall not be a fool; for I will say the truth: but now I forbear, lest any man should think of me above that which he seeth me to be, or that he heareth of me. And he said unto me, My grace is sufficient for thee: for my strength is made perfect in weakness. Most gladly therefore will I rather glory in my infirmities, that the power of Christ may rest upon me. Therefore I take pleasure in infirmities, in reproaches, in necessities, in persecutions, in distresses for Christ's sake: for when I am weak, then am I strong. - 2 Corinthians 12:5-6,9-10

"I am not enough." This may be the most unpopular phrase in today's world. In a society that shouts "You do you"; "You are enough!"; "Do whatever makes you happy!"; "Just believe in yourself"; "Love yourself first so you can love others better"; and my personal favorite, "If Mamma ain't happy, ain't nobody happy."

All of these phrases have something in common. They are all phrases centered around the god of "myself." They are phrases that make everyone else wait in line while you choose to first focus on how you are feeling about yourself. They are phrases that leave God out entirely.

If you are a Christian woman, then you believe that

the God of this Universe created you. He left you a beautiful Book of Guidance so you can know and follow Him. Obeying Him and glorifying Him is what you were created to do. That means our source of truth must come from the Bible. That means we have a filter for all of the latest Facebook memes, commercials, blog posts, catchy songs and movies. Even when that movie makes you feel all warm and fuzzy all over and makes you feel empowered to make something of yourself, we MUST go back to our Source of Truth, God's Word, and see how the message measures up.

One of my least favorite phrases ever is "I Am Enough!" I know that some of your eyes just got bigger and your breathing has changed a little.

But give me a bit to explain. You will never find this phrase in the Bible. You will never find a verse that tells you to love yourself more. You will never even find the principle of loving yourself first. It's just not there.

Why is that? Doesn't Jesus think we are worth it? Maybe it was a phrase lost in translation or something! No, I would gently suggest that you already love yourself and that you are not enough, friend, and neither either am I. (gasp). Can we add even one day to our lives? Can we singlehandedly keep our hearts beating? Can we avoid any bit of heartache that we may face in this life? Are we, in our fallible bodies, our own source of truth? Do we have it all together? Can we get through the death of a loved one in our own strength? Can we save our own souls? Of course not. The answer to all of these questions is a big, huge, "NO!" Thank God the answer is "no!" That leaves a GIANT HOLE that JESUS CHRIST desires to fill.

We are not self-sufficient. We do not have all of the answers. We, simply put, are just not enough. We desperately need a Savior and He is willing to be enough for us because we are not enough on our own. Some of you may point back to the Scripture where Jesus tells us to love our neighbor as ourselves.

I love the way Nancy DeMoss Wolgemuth put it in her book, *Lies Women Believe*, "How often have we heard someone say, 'I've never liked myself' or 'She just doesn't love herself?'" According to the Scripture, the Truth is that we do love ourselves-immensely. When Jesus tells us to love our neighbors as ourselves, the point is not that we need to learn to love ourselves so that we can love others. Jesus is saying we need to give others the same attention and care we naturally give ourselves...So for most of us, our need is not to learn to love ourselves more, but to learn to deny ourselves so we can do that which does not come naturally-love God and others selflessly.

Wow. "Selflessly." Now there's an unpopular word. Friend, to believe that you and I are not enough on our own does NOT give us less value, it does NOT mean we should walk through this life with our heads lowered in shame wishing we could just die. Admitting we are not enough gives us TREMENDOUS value-in Christ. He thought we were worth it. *While we were yet sinners, Christ died for us.*

That is incredible love and a substantial, lasting reason to live.

So what about that person who is struggling with depression or perhaps the one you know who is contemplating suicide? Shouldn't they just be encouraged with the words, "You are enough?" No.

And here's why: Living a life where you just "look inside yourself" for strength is a very. empty. life. It will lead to even more depression and even more suicide because to put it simply-the answers are not found within. You are not enough. You will daily let yourself down and a life lived for you in first place will become a roller coaster of empty, unfulfilling emotions.

You MUST look for Someone Greater to fill that void. Every single day you must "die to yourself" and choose to live for Christ. With this new perspective, "I Am Not Enough," suddenly the huge amount of hours you've been focusing on how you look, how you dress, what the scale reveals and what others are telling you is "put together" pales in comparison to what your eternal mission should be.

Those are not inherently evil things, but they will drop down to lower rankings just as they should. Christ will begin to take preeminence and I can promise you that you will love others more than you ever have. Not because YOU are enough, but because God has been, is and always will be ENOUGH.

My Identity
Rachel Wyatt

Now then we are ambassadors for Christ, as though God did beseech you by us: we pray you in Christ's stead, be ye reconciled to God. - 2 Corinthians 5:20

The African country in which we serve is currently facing some challenging times. As a matter of fact, they were one of the seven countries affected by the recent Covid travel ban issued by the United States. Because of some of these issues, the acting American Ambassador and some of her staff have been traveling to various cities and meeting with the American citizens to discuss some of the challenges. We had the privilege to host them in our home when they came to our city.

As the acting ambassador was speaking to the group of Americans who had gathered, she began telling us how she always tries to stand in a prominent place when ambassadors are being photographed with the president of our country. She explained of how when she is at state functions she behaves in a certain way and when she talks to government officials she speaks in a certain manner. Then she said something that really struck me. She said, "You see, I am not me ... I am the United States of America." As a United States Ambassador, she realizes that every word she speaks, every move she makes, every time she is seen, it is not as herself but rather as The United States of America.

This thought so gripped me as I thought that we, as Christians, are ambassadors for the King of Kings. Every time the world looks at me, they do not see "me" but rather they see a Christian. Every word that I speak, I am telling them, "Hey, this is how Christians speak." Every place that I go, every thing that I wear, every thing that I do is a representation of the God that I serve. Wow! What kind of am ambassador am I?! Am I representing my King well?

As she spoke, I was struck by how her complete identity was not in herself but in the country she represents. We never heard "her" thoughts or "her" opinions, but the thoughts or opinions of the United States government. She had laid aside her own identity (although she is an amazingly smart lady who speaks nine languages!). She has taken upon herself the identity of the country she serves.

I was reminded of a good missionary friend of mine who went to a conference in another African country. At the beginning of the conference, they were doing introductions and she introduced herself, "Hi, I am Ann. I am a missionary with African Inland Mission… " and she went on to list some the projects they were working on. A few other people introduced themselves saying their names and then listing their credentials and organizations that they were working with or works they were doing. This went on for a while until it came time for a group of Ethiopian pastors and workers to introduce themselves. My friend said that she felt so humbled and as these sweet servants of God began to introduce themselves. "Hi, I am John and I am a child of God." "Hi, I am

Mary and I am a child of God." On and on they went around the room all introducing themselves as simply "A child of God."

I know that I am as guilty as the rest at trying to find my identity in something that I do or some title or some great work when, in reality, God simply wants me to be His child! What title could be greater than "A child of God?!" I was challenged to stop seeking an identity in things that I do or acceptance from others or any accomplishments of my own and rest in the fact that my identity is simply that I am a child of God and an ambassador for His cause.

- By Rachel, a child of God

Encouragement From The Men Who Encourage Us

ENCOURAGEMENT FROM WOMEN

Who Am I?
Dr. David Teis

Behold, what manner of love the Father hath bestowed upon us, that we should be called the sons (children) of God: therefore the world knoweth us not, because it knew him not. Beloved, now are we the sons (children) of God, and it doth not yet appear what we shall be: but we know that, when he shall appear, we shall be like him; for we shall see him as he is. And every man that hath this hope in him purifieth himself, even as he is pure. - 1 John 3:1-3

"I am trying to find myself." "I don't know who I am." These expressions became a part of our culture during the social revolution of the 1960s. Many walked away from the God of the Bible and began to embrace eastern mysticism. The eternal realities found in the Word of God slipped from their minds and changed our previously God-centered culture. Without God there are no answers to the great questions surrounding human existence. Thus, many became lost, lacking a purpose for existence.

Questions like "Where did I come from?" "Why am I here?" "Where are we going?" "What is my purpose in life?" went unanswered.

For the Bible savvy Christian, the answers to these questions are relatively obvious.

Why am I here? – Because God created me in His image. Genesis 1:27 provides a clear answer, *So God* *created man in his own image, in the image of God created he him; male and female created he them.*

What is my purpose? – I was created to represent Jesus Christ. 2 Corinthians 5:17 and 20 confirm, *Therefore if any man be in Christ, he is a new creature: old things are passed away; behold, all things are become new. Now then we are ambassadors for Christ, as though God did beseech you by us: we pray you in Christ's stead, be ye reconciled to God.*

Where am I going when I die? – Directly to heaven. 2 Corinthians 5:8 reveals, *We are confident, I say, and willing rather to be absent from the body, and to be present with the Lord.*

Who Am I?
I am a child of the King, living on this planet for one reason. I am here to show people Who Jesus is and introduce them to the Savior. I am an angel (messenger) of God with the message of salvation. I have been given God's truth so I can share the secrets of eternal life with those around me.

The world is confused and rightly so. As a believer, you are not confused and should never be! Live as a born-again child of the King of kings and the Lord of lords. Walk with confidence that He is in control of everything. Know that He has a plan for your life. Never forget that you were adopted into His family. You are royalty – that is who you are!

Your Real Identity
Dr. John R. Van Gelderen

Therefore if any man be in Christ, he is a new creature: old things are passed away; behold, all things are become new. - 2 Corinthians 5:17

Do you know who you are?
What's all new?

Obviously, your body has not been glorified to its new and eternal state. Your soul, though in the process of sanctification, is not yet completely new either. Your soul consists of your mind, emotions, affections, and will. Wrong thinking, bad moods, and poor choices reveal that your soul is not yet all new. But your previously dead spirit has been remarkably restored to life and made marvelously new!

How?

In Christ, the old has departed, the new has come. Most importantly, Christ has moved in. But in order to do so, your human spirit had to be regenerated — changed — to provide a place where He could move in. This is the "new creature" or creation. This part of you is all new. This is the real you — your real identity. How did this occur?

By being placed into Christ, you were placed into His history. This included His death, burial and resurrection. By being identified with Christ in His death, something far reaching occurred in the immaterial part of your being. Your human spirit was severed from the sin master.

The practical essence of death is separation, just as in physical death when the soul separates from the body. Christ died not just for our sins, but unto sin (Romans 6:10). Through death with Christ unto sin, you died to sin (Romans 6:2). Not sins, but sin, the compelling influence inside each of us to commit sins.

The Bible calls this entity *sin that dwelleth in me* (Romans 7:17). Your spirit used to be joined to indwelling sin. But when you were placed into Christ at salvation, your spirit was crucified with Christ and died to (separated from) the old master of indwelling sin. While indwelling sin still seeks to operate in your flesh, at your core you are no longer joined to sin. The relationship has been severed.

Your human spirit died to sin, was raised with Christ, and has been creatively made new. It is described as "the seed [sperma] of God" (1 John 3:9). Amazing!

Something of the very nature of God has been implanted in you. This is the *new man, which after God is created in righteousness and true holiness* (Eph. 4:24).

Your regenerated spirit is righteous and holy! It has to be — it is the Seed of God. And it has to be, because this is where the Holy Spirit resides — in the believer. The old relationship with indwelling sin has been forever severed, and the new relationship with the indwelling Christ has been forever sealed.

This is the real you—righteous. Not merely declared righteous legally, but made righteous actually. *For he hath made him to be sin for us, who knew no sin; that we might be made the righteousness of God in him* (2 Corinthians 5:21). Just as Jesus was "*made…sin*" for us—as a matter of actual fact, we are "*made…righteousness*" in Him—as a matter of actual fact. Amazing!

It is not just positional truth; it is provisional truth that must be accessed by faith in order to be practical truth. But it is actual provision—your spirit is righteous. So give way to the real you!

You are not a loser.

To think you are defeated is the stronghold of the devil's lie. In Christ you are a winner because you are a saint—a holy one. The "seed of God" is not a loser; it is righteous and holy. This is the real you that is joined to the real leader—the indwelling Christ. The real you wants Jesus, loves Jesus, worships Jesus, gives all to Jesus—so give way to the real you.

Go past the noise of the devil's lies, the noise of the soul, the clamor of the world and the flesh, and recognize the far deeper yearnings of your righteous spirit—the real you. Your real response to your real Leader is a righteous response. Take your provision and trust the Spirit to enable you to obey. Live out your real identity as the daughter of the King!

The Most Important Hat of All
Dr. Jeff Redlin

But it shall not be so among you: but whosoever will be great among you, let him be your minister; And whosoever will be chief among you, let him be your servant: Even as the Son of man came not to be ministered unto, but to minister, and to give his life a ransom for many. - Matthew 20:26-28

Hats. You wear a lot of them. While they may not be the "going to church" kind that your grandmother wore, you still wear them. You probably have quite an assortment you are called upon to wear at any given moment. Doctor, chauffer, friend, fashion designer, psychologist, protector, cheerleader, taskmaster, and sometimes even a hero!

With so many hats, a person can struggle to know who he or she really is. Have you considered the contradiction of roles that Jesus Himself entered into when He left the splendors of Heaven and came to earth as … a man?

Think about it. The One who is the Bread of Life officially began His ministry hungering for 40 days in the wilderness being tempted of the devil. The One Who is Living Water ended His ministry saying, "I thirst." Yes, Christ hungered as man, and yet fed the hungry as God. He thirsted as a man, yet is Living Water to all who will drink. He was weary as a man yet offers rest to all who will come to Him. He stumbled under the weight of the cross yet bears the weight of the world upon His shoulders. He wept at the funeral of Lazarus yet is the One Who wipes away our tears. He was sentenced to death by the Roman government yet is the One Who established human government. He was led as a sheep to the slaughter, but is the Good Shepherd. He died, and yet He ever lives. This is but the tip of the iceberg when we consider the mystery of the God-Man, Jesus Christ. Born in a stable, yet came as the King. No place to lay His head, yet He is the Head of all.

If ever there was a person who could have had a crisis of identity, it was Jesus. Was He rich or poor, servant or sovereign, friend or foe, weak or mighty ... God or man?

The very Author of our faith submitted Himself to the rugged storyline of humanity and took on the role of the "Man of Sorrows." And while Jesus wore with absolute grace every "hat" He was called upon to wear, He never lost sight of Whom He truly was and what He was called to do. Yes, He knew He was God, but He willingly took upon Him the "form of a servant." When you boil it all down, this was the thread that ran through every hat He ever wore ... He came to serve ... to give His life a ransom for many.

You are called upon every day to wear a lot of hats. Jesus wore many as well—even hats that appeared to be contradictory to the person He truly is. But there was one hat He never removed. It gave clarity, focus, purpose and meaning to everything He did. It was His servant hat. We know He came as our example.

So, He invites us to wear the hat that He wore well. In fact, it looks good on us also. It truly is, of the many hats we wear, the most important hat of all.

… by love serve one another. (Galatians 5:13)

Don't Always Let Your Conscience Be Your Guide
By Matthew Teis

And there came a voice to him, Rise, Peter; kill, and eat. But Peter said, Not so, Lord; for I have never eaten any thing that is common or unclean. And the voice spake unto him again the second time, What God hath cleansed, that call not thou common. - Acts 10:13-15

Would God ever ask someone to violate her or his own conscience? The answer of course is yes!

After expecting to have an heir to the promise of God for years, God honored Abraham's faithfulness by blessing him with a son, Isaac. Years pass, God commands Abraham to sacrifice his son.

Did it make sense? Was this the plan of God?

I am sure there were some struggles with adhering to the command of God. Maybe this command violated his conscience. Bible students know how God demonstrated His provision and never exacted this duty from Abraham, but he was less concerned with Abraham's conscience and more interested in him following His commands.

When Moses takes the mantle of leader for the Israelite people God requires an awkward practice of circumcision to be performed on his son. In Exodus 4:25, his wife, Zipporah, expresses her disdain for the practice by calling Moses a bloody man. It violated her conscience, but Moses followed the command.

Peter's involvement in the centurion brings a believer to the same crossroads. His conscience forbade eating unclean meats. He argues with God three times about the command, but submits. His conscience is violated, but the command is followed. Cultural heritage, patriotism, and religious practices build up a conscience barrier in our lives. Often, these matters of conscience promote a healthy walk with God. But many times we can wrap our identity in what our conscience urges us to do instead of securing our identity in who Christ is in our lives.

There is a place of conflict when our conscience fails to align with the clear commands of God. Peter felt that tension and appealed to God to relieve the tension and was denied. Peter didn't allow this to shake his faith in who He was in Jesus.

The Disciple of Christ must consider their conscience. Romans 14:22 clearly states, *Hast thou faith? have it to thyself before God. Happy is he that condemneth not himself in that thing which he alloweth.*

God may use our conscience, but maturity in Christ heeds the Holy Spirit and differentiates between conscience and conviction. Conscience allows cultural Christianity to rest in the ease of standards and check lists. The commands of Christ break out the stale parade of religion and unleash the power of the Holy Spirit through relationship. Peter wisely violated his conscience for the command of God. In doing so, he demonstrated his reliance on Who Christ is and his relationship with Him.

The Enemy is a Liar!
By Samson Correa

Therefore if any man be in Christ, he is a new creature: old things are passed away; behold, all things are become new.
– 2 Corinthians 5:17

My alarm goes off at 4:30 am. I hate it. I want to hit the snooze button. The truth is every now and then I do. I feel guilty afterwards. Was it worth it I ask? No. Not really.

The problem is that growing up I struggled with my image. My self esteem. Tall. Very skinny. No matter what I did. No matter what I eat. (Poor me I know) Mentally it has always been a very real problem. Mentally, emotionally. To make matters worse my parents gave me the name Samson.

I was at the gym this morning working out. Every time I look in the mirror, in my mind, I still see the image. Tall skinny. No matter how much effort I exhert lifting weights...no matter how dedicated I am. As I sat there the Spirit of God laid this upon my heart. How many Christians think like this. They minister ... serve the Lord ... they look in the mirror and are frustrated ... why? Because they still see themselves as the unsaved unregenerate person.

As I sat in the gym, an image flashed in my mind. Me 10 years ago. There he is. The image of myself that I hated. The Spirit of God spoke to my heart as I meditated on that old image of myself. You're not that person anymore. You look different.

I don't know who needs to hear this, but our Enemy wants you to believe that you are too spiritually weak, skinny and frail. He wants you to think that the more you serve... the more you minister... the more you try to draw close to the Lord ... in prayer ... in reading His Word ... no matter how dedicated you become ... going to services in person ... listening to sermons online throughout the week. He wants you to believe that you will fail.

Here's the truth... are you ready? Let the Spirit of God speak to your heart as He does to mine. Imagine who you were before you came to Christ...

(take a moment to pause and reflect), now, look at the person that you have become ... spiritually ... you are not the same person. Take a moment in prayer... thank God for His mercy and grace and remember, the deceiver is a LIAR!

An Invitation to Contribute

We at EFW are always looking for inspiring authors who seek to encourage others in their walk with the Lord.

Please visit encouragementfromwomen.com if you would like to submit a devotional that would appear on our social media accounts.

✉EFW@experienceliberty.com

⊙encouragementfromwomen

f EncouragementFromWomenWhoveBeenThere

Author Biographies
(Organized Alphabetically)

Sarah Adler
Sarah resides in New Britain, Connecticut where she actively serves in her local church. She enjoys singing with the worship team, reading, and discipling new believers. Sarah has a preteen daughter, is employed in medical administration, and is currently pursuing a career in nursing.

Joanna Alipalo
Joanna resides in Vancouver, British Columbia where she works as a teacher in a Christian school. She moved to Canada from the Philippines when she was 16, and surrendered her life to full time ministry when she was 18. She loves to travel, sing, and read. She serves God in whatever opportunity is given — big or small.

Charity Berkey
Charity is the founder of Encouragement From Women Who've Been There [EFW]. The EFW website and social media platforms provide daily biblical encouragement and resources for woman around the globe. Currently the EFW social media pages actively reach over 240,000 followers. Charity resides in her hometown of Las Vegas where she and her husband, Neal, have served on staff at Liberty Baptist Church for the past seventeen years. Though she loves serving in various ministries, Charity's favorite

calling continues to be her role as wife to Neal and homeschool mama to their four children, Tre, Cherish, Lincoln, and Felicity.

Alana Brown
Alana is the Senior Pastor's wife at West Florida Baptist Church in Milton, Florida, where she serves with her husband and four children. Being highly involved in the church and school ministry, she leads the ladies ministry. She also mentors, counsels, and is a speaker to ladies of all ages. She loves theater, chocolate, coffee, and most of all, shoes!

Tamah Bryant
Tamah lives Southwest of Tucson, Arizona, with her husband and three sons. She has three older children who are married and three adorable granddaughters. She ministers in the jail on the Reservation and in her parents mission church. She is currently working as a sub in the community's local public school where God continues to give opportunities for her to share the love and hope of the gospel of Jesus with some pretty amazing kids. God has used her work in the public school to start a small group ministry. They meet with kids once a week. You can keep up with how the Lord is working in her life on undefeatedinchrist.blogspot.com.

Irene Castaneda
Irene grew up in Las Vegas and has been attending Liberty Baptist Church for as long as she can remember. She enjoys spending time with family and friends; exploring new places; hiking; watching sunsets on the beach; and drinking lots of coffee. She

recently graduated from College with a Bachelor of Science degree in Elementary Education and desires to serve the Lord in Christian education.

Shelley Conway
Shelley serves in full-time ministry with her husband, Larry. They served for 25 years at Ironwood Christian Camp in Southern California before transitioning to working full time with Nehemiah Corps, a service ministry to camps and the churches that support those camps. Shelley is a cancer survivor, mother of three adult children, and encourager to all she meets.

Kimberly Coombes
Kimberly is a wife, mother of four, musician, blogger, and daily disciple of Christ. She serves alongside her husband on staff at Southern Hills Baptist Church as part of the worship team, and has an outreach for sexually abused women seeking healing from past trauma. You can join her for a winsome conversation in all things wisdom, worship, and womanhood in her weekly blog setinsilver.org.

Samson Correa
Born in Brooklyn, raised in Queens, Samson is no stranger to how difficult our lives can be without knowing who we are in Jesus Christ. At the age of 25, God brought he and his now wife to Liberty Baptist Church in Las Vegas, Nevada. It was there they both trusted Christ as Savior. For over a decade Samson and his wife have faithfully served in various ministries together ranging from children's and youth ministry to adult discipleship.

Kelly Edmondson
Kelly is the Co-Founder and Medical Director of Medical Missions Outreach. She and her husband, Bradley, travel the globe sharing Jesus with those who need both medical help and spiritual healing. She, her husband, and four children base their ministry out of Georgia.

Sierra V. Fedorko
Sierra lives in a bright blue house with her family, dog, goats, and chickens. (Well, the goats and chickens live outside!) She and her husband, Ben, serve at Wolf Mountain Christian Camp. She blogs regularly at sierrafedorko.com with a focus on poetry, telling the stories they have lived through a lens of healing, hope, and beauty. Sierra recently published Hope Gives a Eulogy, a collection of 96 poems exploring how her own journey of infertility impacted her faith, friendships, womanhood, and marriage. You can find Hope Gives a Eulogy on Amazon alongside her first book, A Pygmy's Life for Me, an autobiography with fictional elements as she retells stories from her childhood and teenage years and shares her discovery of freedom in Christ from the "good girl" perception and her chronic pain.

Mindy Flanagan
Mindy has been married to, Aaron, the man of her dreams, for 19 years and counting. She is the blessed mom to four amazing kids: Madison, Riley, Brynlee, and Elijah. She has been the Lead Pastor's wife at Oasis Baptist Church of Las Vegas for the last eight years.

Grace Hayes

Grace is a Pastor's wife living overseas; mom to two boys; and friend to many. Her passion is connecting with and encouraging women to live out their identity through the gospel via one-on-one mentoring and group discipleship.

Melody Holloway

Melody has a Masters in Psychology, and she has worked with youth for 13+ years. She is currently living and working in Casa Grande, AZ, as a school counselor. She also conducts a ministry at New Life Baptist Church. She loves working with her students, teaching the Bible, reading, spending time with family, drinking tea, and cooking.

Jennifer Holmes

Jennifer is a wife, mom, speaker, and writer who also happens to have Bipolar II and she's exploring how mental health and faith intersect. She has over ten years experience teaching the Bible, a Biblical Counselling certificate from CCEF, and is currently working on her master's in Biblical Counselling at Westminster Theological Seminary. You can find her most often on Instagram and she has resources waiting for you on her website. Her book, Hope That Outlasts The Ashes, is a study on the book of Job and is available on Amazon.

McKenzie Jones

McKenzie, her husband Phillip, and their three boys worked as a team and started Crosspoint Baptist Church in Pasadena, CA, in September of 2016. With all of the wild experiences, exciting stories, and an immense love for the Bible, McKenzie has a passion to encourage ladies in their day-to-day lives as they search for the meaning of life, ask the tough questions, or are already a growing Christian desiring to just get closer to Jesus. Her greatest desire is to show others this life can only truly be lived to the fullest as we are, *Strengthened with all might, according to his glorious power...* Colossians 1:11. You can find out more about her and her ministry at withallmight.com.

Kimberly Joy
Kimberly lives in the Missouri Ozarks with her three nearly-grown sons and enjoys writing stories, and devotionals at www.kimberlyjoyauthor.com. She is the author of *Tales from Toddlers*, a 30-day devotional book based on true adventures with the little tykes in her home daycare. It can be found on Amazon.

Shonda Kuehl
Shonda is married to her best friend, Cody. Her husband is the Lead Pastor of Grand Rapids Baptist Church in Grand Rapids, Michigan. Together they love serving Jesus and going on adventures with their four kids!

Jen McGee
Jen is a forgiven and loved child of God, a Pastor's wife in the great state of Texas and a mom to five beautiful kids. Feel free to check out her blog "Just a Mom's View" at juniperjen4jesus.net.

Blandy Mendoza
Blandy is a wife to John and mom to Justin, Jacob, Josiah, and Jaiden. She has served the Lord in full time church and camp ministry along side her husband for 17 years. She has a passion for singing, reading, and teaching God's Word to women. Follow her on Facebook: Blandy Mendoza, Instagram: @Blandy, and visit her websites: Blandymusic.com and Lomadevida.org.

Courtney Holloway Montgomery
A South Carolina native, Courtney Montgomery taught history in Hawaii for five years after attending college in Florida. An internship at a Washington, D.C. based educational nonprofit led to a staff role as a legislative assistant. As a representative for an association of private, K-12 Christian schools, she wrote a weekly newsletter for their constituency; met with Members and Hill staffers about legislative issues; coordinated national conferences for state leaders and politically interested students; and spoke at teachers' conferences around the country. She primarily monitored issues such as Common Core, school choice, and religious liberty. In 2014, she married Chris, a police officer, and moved back to South Carolina. Her love for politics and social media led to the start of The Cerebral Conservative Facebook group blog and Instagram. In 2020, she was a visiting fellow with the Independent Women's Forum and served as a consultant to an international missions agency. She currently works in public relations at a university. Courtney enjoys documenting her food and travel experiences with her husband on her blog, Yeah That Courtney,

consuming copious amounts of news, taking photos of everything in sight, and spending time with her family.

Lysandra Osterkamp
Lysandra is a passionate follower of Jesus. She is a speaker, storyteller, teacher, pod caster, woman's and marriage counselor, and author. She is married to her childhood sweetheart Thomas Osterkamp, Lead Pastor at Beachside Community Church, Palm Coast, Florida. They have been serving God in pastoral ministry for 18 years. Lysandra and Thomas homeschool their four beautiful, spunky, funny girls: Kathryne, Isabella, Abigail, and Violet. Their house is always busy, dramatic, exciting, and full of love. Her book, "Balancing the Crazy" is available on Amazon and kindle. Her podcasts, "Family Meeting" and "Everyday Christian Mom" can be found on most podcast providers. Please visit her website at, lysandraosterkamp.com. You can find her on Facebook at, Lysandra Osterkamp Motivational Speaker.

Denise Peterson
Denise has served along side her husband for the past 41 years at First Baptist Church of Land O'Lakes, Florida. They love their two grown children and especially their five adorable grandchildren. As the lead pastor's wife, Denise enjoys planning their church's mission trips; Good News Clubs; and ladies' functions, as well as teaching saxophone lessons and playing in a sax quartet with her students.

Sharon Rabon

Sharon grew up in a Christian home in Midland City, Alabama. She trusted Christ as her Savior and gave her life to serve the Lord in lifetime ministry as a teenager. Sharon married her high school sweetheart, Tim Rabon, on July 27, 1997. In 1981 they were asked to join the staff of Beacon Baptist Church in Raleigh, NC. In 1997, her husband became the pastor of that church. Sharon is director of ladies' ministries and serves as her husband's secretary. She has written two 60 day devotional books entitled Pause and Selah. You can purchase those on her website, www.sharonrabon.com, as well as find other helpful resources. She is the mom of two sons and one daughter, all of whom are married and serve in lifetime ministry. Her favorite role is being Nana to eight Cute Kids.

Dr. Jeff Redlin

Dr. Redlin was saved at the age of seventeen. Realizing God was calling him into full-time vocational Christian ministry he attended Pensacola Christian College. He and his wife Julie were married in 1992 and have faithfully served the Lord together in various ministries. Currently, Dr. Redlin serves as the Senior Pastor of the Campus Church of Pensacola Christian College in Pensacola Florida.

Emily Sealy

Emily lives in Canada with her husband of 16 years and her four children, whom she homeschools. She and her husband were in church ministry for the first 11 years of their marriage. Emily has had a lifetime of health issues which eventually led to her losing the use of her legs and becoming a full-time wheelchair user in 2018. Emily loves to write, and uses that love to write about life in a wheelchair and the challenges that brings, as well as all that God is teaching her in day-to-day life. Her passion is to encourage others. While life may be hard, God is always good. You can read more of her writings on her blog at www.emilysealy.com.

Jennifer Selver
Jennifer would describe herself as an imperfect woman striving to serve The Perfect King! She gave her life to The Lord as a young child, yet continues to seek after the knowledge of God in her adult years. She developed a desire to serve The Lord in ministry during her teen years. She is passionate about ministering to women in various seasons of their lives. Jennifer has been faced with many challenges, but is forever thankful for God's amazing grace that carries her through! Jennifer is the wife of Evangelist Kwame Selver. They reside in Nassau, Bahamas.

Fun Facts about Jennifer: She loves playing games and is very very very very competitive. She enjoys reading—real books, e-books, blog posts, social media posts, directions, instruction manuals, and even all of the fine print on advertisements and medications. To hear more from Jennifer, follow her on Instagram: @FOCUSladies or contact her through Email at: jen.selver@gmail.com.

Dawn Suttle
Dawn has been married 37 years to, Vern, the love of her life. She is a church secretary, youth leader, Mom

of four, Grandma of seven. She enjoys life and finding joy.

Dr. David Teis
Dr. Teis is the founder and lead pastor of Liberty Baptist Church of Las Vegas. Together, he and his wife Anna have served in ministry for over 45 years. He is the father of five children, grandfather to eighteen. Currently he and Anna travel across the country encouraging pastors and their families while hosting Family Life, Mission's and Prayer Conferences. To inquire about booking Dr. Teis for a conference or purchasing one of his most recent books, please visit DavidTeis.com.

Matthew Teis
Matthew is the Executive Pastor of Liberty Baptist Church of Las Vegas. Together, he and his wife Breanna have served in ministry for over 20 years. He is the father of four children, Ashlynne, Bethany, Charlotte and Luke.

Amanda Thorne
Amanda is a Pastor's wife from Decatur, Texas. She has two boys on earth and one precious boy in heaven. If she could give one piece of advice it would be to allow God's grace to overflow through your life and share it with those around you. Grace was never meant to be hoarded. Follow her on Instagram at lipsticklunges_andgrace.

Dr. John R. Van Gelderen
Dr. Van Gelderen entered full-time evangelism in 1992 and has preached throughout the United States

and in twenty foreign countries. John is the president of Revival Focus Ministries, an organization for the cause of revival and evangelism, and preaches in revival meetings and conferences internationally. He has written eight books as well as many tracts and songs and is active on his blog at revivalfocus.org. John holds BA and MA degrees in Bible and doctorate in pastoral theology. He travels with his wife, Mary Lynn and their son John Jr., in revival ministry and is based out of Ann Arbor, Michigan.

Tamara Weatherbee
Tamara is a stay-at-home mom to her three little ones. She truly enjoys being able to stay home with her children but also work from home. She is a social media influencer where she loves to empower and validate women all over the world. Tamara and her husband, Anthony, have served at Lighthouse Baptist Church in Gulf breeze Florida where her husband has been the Assistant Pastor for 7 years. You can connect with Tamara on Instagram @tamara_weatherbee, Facebook tamara_weatherbee, Tiktok @tamara_weatherbee.

Christi Wells
Christi is a public speaker, writer, and educator who is currently following God's calling to homeschool her children. She is the former Prevention Director for Refuge For Women, a national organization fighting human sex trafficking. She resides in Richmond, KY, with her husband, Kyle, and their four children. They love Jesus, own a Chick-fil-A, and travel as much as possible, sharing their journeys on their travel blog: @wellsfamilytravels. To learn more about Refuge and

the fight to end sex slavery, go to
http://www.rfwky.org/.

Kathy Whittenburg
Kathy is the mother of four awesome kiddos. She's
been married to Andrew, the Pastor of Faith Baptist
Church in Plymouth, WI, for 15 years. She has a deep
love of coffee, making her bed everyday, and her least
favorite chore is doing laundry. She was saved at 16
years of age during summer camp. Her favorite verse
is Psalm 63:8, *My soul followeth hard after thee: thy right
hand upholdeth me.*

Cindy Mainous Wicks
Cindy is the mamma to three amazing kids and
serves along side of her husband, Joseph, with
Medical Missions Outreach. They offer medical,
dental, optical, and physical therapy clinics to people
in developing countries all across the world in order
to share the Gospel of Christ.

Stephanie Willard
Stephanie lives in Rocky Mount, NC, where she
enjoys serving in ministry with her pastor-husband,
Michael, and being a momma to their three children.
She's passionate about empowering and encouraging
women to live abundantly and authentically through
volunteer work at her local crisis pregnancy center,
and in her role as a health and wellness advocate. She
enjoys reading, music, fitness, and coffee!

Rachel Wyatt
Rachel and her husband, Jerry, have been serving as missionaries to Tanzania, East Africa for the past 14 years. God has blessed them with four beautiful children all of whom were born in Tanzania. Rachel fills her days homeschooling the oldest two and cleaning up after the younger two. She assists Jerry in the various aspects of the ministry and women's ministries. In her "spare time" she enjoys graphic design. You can learn more about their work on their website: www.wyatttanzania.com.

Faith York
Faith is blessed to be called wife, mama, and very loved child of God. She's a singer, songwriter and pianist. She loves to read, watch sunsets, and eat chocolate. Singing with her family is at the top of the list, though. She also blogs at andwithmysong.com and would love you to join her. Her heart is to encourage the discouraged and her deepest desire is that everything she does or says brings glory to Jesus only. He has been enough and she wants to spend every breath praising Him (Psalm 28:7). "It is not enough to have a song on your lips. You must also have a song in your heart." - Fanny Crosby

Bethany Young
Bethany is a composer, artist, writer, and ministry wife. Her passion is to inspire others to meditate on God's Word and live for eternity. You can find her book, "Burn Out or Be Still," at creativityministry.com or follow her on social media @creativityministry.

Additional Resources

Teis Talks

Teis Talks: it's more than a conversation! Teis Talks is a fun conversation that provides biblical and practical application to the problems of your every day life.

Looking for a long lasting, love filled marriage? Desiring to raise children who love Jesus? Look no further than Teis Talks.

You will find many of the same authors on EFW being interviewed on Teis Talks.

Encouragement For Women

Encouragement For Women is our first devotional book produced by EFW.

This 30 day devotional has a range of topics dealing with friendship, forgiveness and hope for every day living. A perfect read for every Christian woman. Order yours today on Amazon.

A Final Word

Who am I? Why am I here? Where am I going?

The above questions have been asked for centuries. Commoners, educators and philosophers have all desired to answer these ever pressing questions yet when we seek to answer them aside from God's Word, we remain lost.

But God desires you to be found. He not only answers these questions, but he wants you to know the future. He desires you to know where you will spend eternity.

No matter your experience, God has a true purpose for your life. He also desires that you make Heaven your eternal home with Him. His home is no fantasy, in fact, His Son left earth with the promise of creating a home for those who place their faith and trust in Him. His gift to you is eternal life in Heaven along with Him. God the Father paid for this home in Heaven by sending His Son, Jesus Christ.

Jesus cares about everyone! In fact, He cared about us so much that 2,000 years ago, He left the glory of Heaven to come to earth so that He could give us the gift of eternal life. The question is, how can we get this gift?

Have you ever told a lie, lost your temper, taken something that didn't belong to you? We all have. The Bible calls the breaking of God's law – sin.

For all have sinned, and come short of the glory of God: - Romans 3:23

Our sin separates us from God, and must be paid for. *For the wages of sin is death; but the gift of God is eternal life through Jesus Christ our Lord.* - Romans 6:23

Now for the good news…Jesus Christ willingly was crucified, buried, and rose from the dead in order to pay for our sins. *Christ died for our sins according to the scriptures; And that he was buried, and that he rose again the third day according to the scriptures.* – 1 Corinthians 15:3-4

God allowed this because He is actively pursuing our hearts. *But God commendeth his love toward us, in that, while we were yet sinners, Christ died for us.* – Romans 5:8

Jesus desires that you be found. He offers us an eternal life in Heaven if we simply believe on Him for salvation. We demonstrate this belief by calling on Him. *That if thou shalt confess with thy mouth the Lord Jesus, and shalt believe in thine heart that God hath raised him from the dead, thou shalt be saved…For whosoever shall call upon the name of the Lord shall be saved.* - Romans 10:9, 13

If you've placed your trust in Christ after reading this you are officially part of the family of God! You have purpose, you have meaning, and you now have a future in Heaven. You may have questions and we would love to answer them. Please contact us so we can celebrate with you!

You were once lost, but now you are found! Your future is bright!

Made in the USA
Middletown, DE
30 December 2021

57330172R00102